Crossings 41

SEMPRE FIDELE

All rights reserved. Parts of this book may be reprinted only by written permission from the author, and may not be reproduced for publication in book, magazine, or electronic media of any kind, except in quotations for purposes of literary reviews by critics.

© 2024, Joseph Bathanti
© 2024, "'*Contar y cantar*': The Other Voice of Poetry" and translation by Marina Morbiducci
© 2024, "A Tour of Bathanti Country" and translation by Darcy Di Mona

Cover photograph: "Meadow Street Bridge" from Pittsburgh City Photographer Collection, 1901-2000, Archives Service Center, University of Pittsburgh.

Library of Congress Control Number: 2024942522

Published by
BORDIGHERA PRESS
John D. Calandra Italian American Institute
25 W. 43rd Street, 17th Floor
New York, NY 10036

Crossings 41
ISBN 978-1-59954-224-9

Sempre Fidele

and other poems

a bilingual edition

Joseph Bathanti

Introduced and translated
by Marina Morbiducci
and Darcy Di Mona

BORDIGHERA PRESS

*To our own transatlantic friendship today
and to all the transatlantic crossings before us.*

Table of Contents

Restituted	9
"*Contar y cantar*": the Other Voice of Poetry	14
A Tour of Bathanti Country	23
Paolo Mio / *Paolo mio*	42
Sempre Fidele / *Sempre fedele*	46
Larimer Avenue / *Larimer Avenue*	58
The Headstone / *La lapide*	62
A Better Life / *Miglior vita*	66
Graziella / *Graziella*	70
Lincoln Avenue / *Lincoln Avenue*	72
Prometheus / *Prometeo*	76
Son of a Priest / *Figlio di un prete*	80
Confirmation / *Cresima*	84
Kyrie / *Kyrie*	88
The Hollow / *Lo Sprofondo*	92
The Witch / *La strega*	96
The Death of East Liberty / *La morte di East Liberty*	100
The Strike Baby / *Il Bambino dello sciopero*	102
Mendicant on a Bridge / *Mendicante sul ponte*	106
This Metal / *Questo metallo*	110
Turns / *Turni*	114
Mayday / *Allarme 1° maggio*	118
Aunt Nina in Midair / *Zia Nina sospesa in aria*	120
Saint Marie Street / *Saint Marie Street*	126
From the Photograph of the Church Steps: September 3, 1947 / *Dalla fotografia della scalinata della chiesa, il 3 settembre 1947*	130
The Tongue / *La lingua*	136
The Electrifying Vernacular of Escape / *L'elettrizzante vernacolo della fuga*	140
Silence / *Silenzio*	144
Eggplant / *Melanzana*	146
Maria Roselina / *Maria Roselina*	148
Domenico Giuseppe / *Domenico Giuseppe*	152
My Father's Hat / *Il cappello di mio padre*	156
The Huckster / *Il venditore ambulante*	158
The DeNinno Sisters / *Le sorelle DeNinno*	162

High Mass / *Messa della domenica*	166
Braciole / *Involtini*	170
Concertina / *Concertina*	172
For Frank O'Hara / *Per Frank O'Hara*	176
Light at the Seam / *Luce alla vena*	178
Limbo / *Limbo*	180
Acknowledgments	183
About the Author	185
About the Translators	187

Restituted

On Sunday, November 6, 2016, I received an email from Marina Morbiducci, a professor of English Language and Translation at Sapienza University in Rome. Among Marina's many areas of literary expertise is her formidable scholarship on Black Mountain College and she has written extensively on the poets and poetics of Black Mountain. She had come across my work on Black Mountain and extended an invitation to contribute a batch of my poems to a forthcoming issue of *RSAJournal*, the literary publication associated with AISNA (Associazione Italiana Studi Nord-Americani), in which Prof. Morbiducci planned to curate a forum, titled "Black Mountain College: Revisited."

Of course, I was powerfully flattered and sent along the poems, which Marina graciously accepted. She then proposed an interview with me, at the heart of which, ultimately, was my Italian American identity and its overwhelming and unmistakable influence as a wellspring for my writing. In the very last of her incisive and probing questions, she asked me to reflect on what she termed a "double consciousness" in the two poles of my identity—Italian and American—and my perception of how that dynamic comes into play in my process of composition.

I confessed in my response that "I often feel like an impostor—a bit of a poseur as I have at my disposal only a handful of Italian words . . . " That said, I also confessed that "once I realized that my central trove—my primary preoccupation, the subject matter I was most passionate about and would never be exhausted—was indeed my Italian American heritage, my writing and my confidence as a writer took a quantum leap."

But the question persists: Do those two identities—"typically Italian and typically American," as Marina phrased it—"coexist harmoniously" or is there, indeed, "a sense of double consciousness?" I replied in the interview that "My reflex is to say that the two identities are seamless, inseparable, but I'm not sure that is true. What I do know is who I am is immutably shaped by ancestry . . . " and the fact that I grew up in a Little Italy in Pittsburgh that was utterly and unapologetically saturated with *italianità*. However, it wasn't until I read *Beyond the Godfather: Italian American Writers on the Real Italian American Experience*, edited by A. Kenneth Ciongoli and Jay Parini, and witnessed in its pages iterations of my lived life, that I realized I was not only an Italian American writer, but that a rich and storied tradition of Italian American literature existed. That book gave me the permission to write what I knew best, what I am able to authenticate—exclusively in English—and am most passionate about. But there remains, perhaps, another level of authenticity I aspire to: the Italian language and how my thoroughly American prose and verse articulates into it.

By the time *RSAJournal* #28, 2017, with my poems and the interview, was published, Marina and I had been corresponding regularly. In that lovely and serendipitous vein that friendship is forged from the virtual correspondence of two people who have never crossed paths in the flesh, we found ourselves fast friends—and it bears mention that we are exactly the same age, born on the very same day.

On another Sunday—June 25, 2017—Marina suggested the prospect of a collaboration, which we had both kept alive in our discussions: a bilingual edition of select poems of mine. She mentioned that, as a translator, she remains "curious . . . to get into the compositional process" of an author and "restitute it into the other language." I was most intrigued, in this instance, by "restitute"—which means "to restore to a former state or position," to "give back," to "refund." I loved that notion. It smacked of expiation and concomitant exoneration. A translation into Italian of my American poems, written in English, struck me as a version of atonement, reparation—perhaps authentication, even sacramental. I would be translated, reconstituted, into a real Italian. Marina also stated her joy in "transmuting the original text into poetical Italian," yet staying true to "the author's intention." *Transmutation* suggests a kind of alchemy that also intrigues me: translation as a kind of magic in which the translator also performs as medium—though I don't wish to over-mystify the very real, painstaking, often deviling labor that literary translation demands.

Marina and I continued to correspond, fairly steadily, over the next two and a half years—about our work and shared interest in Black Mountain College, children, dogs, politics and weather; but in the main we talked about literature, poetry in particular, and sporadic allusions to our dream of collaborating on a translation of my poems.

On February 21, 2020, the first patient in Italy was diagnosed with Covid-19, and a lockdown across the country was instituted on March 9. As the pandemic gained traction worldwide, Italy's active Covid cases remained one of the highest in the world. Soon, the entire planet was preoccupied by the pandemic, though of course no one dreamed how seemingly interminable and lethal it would prove. I had been scheduled to be in Italy the summer of 2020, and Marina and I had planned to lay the groundwork for the translation project then.

In September of 2020, when it became shockingly evident that the pandemic would not permit my travel to Italy that year, and quite possibly the next, 2021, I broached the possibility of launching our translation discussions via Zoom. At that juncture, teachers world-wide, including Marina and me, had been suddenly saddled with teaching online and, before we knew it, we and our students had been absorbed into the realm of Zoom. Thus, by dint of a devastating pandemic, Marina and I suddenly had a platform congenial to the kind of face-to-face, intimate conversations crucial to the art of translation.

Marina had earlier suggested adding to our collaboration, her colleague, Professor Darcy Di Mona, a New York City native, fluent in Italian, a teacher and professional translator over an amazingly wide range of the arts, who has spent nearly forty years in Italy, and conducted a translation workshop for four years at Sapienza University. Marina's brilliant rationale: "I usually consult a native speaker to check that my interpretation is correct."

Marina and I decided that an intelligent, logical point of departure would be a focus on poems I'd written that explored my sense of *italianità* and my own intersection, from the cradle, with my immigrant ancestry, growing up in a very old-world, Italian immigrant neighborhood, the grandson of Italian immigrants, and being very much a part of that culture—the culture that ignites so very much of my writing. We agreed that we would allow the collaboration to take shape organically, unfettered by too many preconceived expectations. In February of 2021, I sent Marina a selection of poems and, on June 14, we staged our inaugural Zoom meeting, just Marina and I, at 10 a.m my time, 4 p.m. hers.

Marina and I met weekly, and then Darcy joined us on July 12. She instantly proved utterly invaluable, as Marina had assured me. I, of course, hadn't considered how perplexing American English, even regional, colloquialisms, slang, and coined terms would be to a non-native translator. Understandably, Marina—who, by my lights, is an absolute wonder when it comes to reading, writing and speaking English—was thoroughly stumped by certain language in my poems that Darcy termed *Americana*: "broads" for women; "heap" for car; "porch gliders" for those old-fashioned love seats that swung back and forth on rails like a rocking chair; "craps" for the street-gambling dice game; "needle" as a synonym for "antagonize." Along with her elegant command of the Italian language, Darcy brought her NYC street acumen to the table.

Fittingly, the first translation completed was of "Paolo Mio," what I still conceive of as my first good poem, its initial draft written in 1981 at my parents' dining room table in Pittsburgh, where I grew up.

To date, Marina, Darcy and I have met, transatlantically, via Zoom, fifty times, ninety minutes per session—and it's impossible to gauge the hours we've spent together via email over the past nineteen months—in a collaboration that ineluctably hatched from that very first email from Marina, all the way back on Nov. 6, 2016, and resulted in *Sempre Fidele & Other Poems*.

Collaborating with Marina and Darcy has allowed me to reconsider my own poetics in wholly new and invigorating ways. Their brilliance and blue-collar work ethic—their great friendship and the abiding love that developed among us—made my poems come to life all over again—*restituted, transmuted*, in Italian, and have led me to reimagine my method of composition in English in wholly new and illuminating ways.

More than anything, hearing from their mouths the translations of my poems—the aural splendor of the Italian language that chanted the glorious refrain of my early life among my Italian grandparents and the old Italian people in the neighborhood—the language I was regaled by from my earliest moments on earth—has been perhaps the greatest gift of all. So moving. A thrill. My gratitude has no bounds.

JOSEPH BATHANTI
Vilas, North Carolina
February 25, 2023

"*Contar y cantar*": the Other Voice of Poetry

PREAMBLE

Translating the poetry of Joseph Bathanti has been an invaluable experience of personal and professional growth. The close encounter with his poems created the occasion for a reappraisal both of the task of the literary translator and the role of the Translation Studies scholar. Plunging into the forms and content of Joseph Bathanti's texts, I could immerse myself deeply, sometimes breathlessly, in the immense and abyssal beauty of poetical language. The dialogue between the poet and his/her translator is always a mysterious path, constellated by unexpected turns and surprising solutions, whereby the two languages are mutually enhanced. The intense hours of work together generated a few reflections on the poetical voice in general, but particularly on Joseph Bathanti's, which I'm glad to share in the following preamble to *Sempre Fidele and Other Poems*.

THE OTHER VOICE

"Contar y cantar (sobre el poema extenso)" is the opening essay contained in the collection of poetry criticism titled *La otra voz*, which Octavio Paz published in 1990 (the same year when he was awarded the Nobel Prize for Literature) and in which the voice element is pivotal to the creation of the "poema extenso," as clarified in the subtitle. The dyptich "Contar y cantar" in Spanish ("to narrate" and "to sing") presents a play on words (specifically paronomasia), and in this simple apophonic change of vowel (from "o" to "a") a whole universe is encapsulated: when you recount and sing, the epic form comes spontaneously to the surface, springing from the urge to render in words the multiple human experiences (and Paz—quoting in his epigraph Antonio Machado: "Se canta una viva historia / contando su melodía"—beautifully expands such a concept, swirling from Mahabarata to Homer, from Dante to Milton, from Ariosto to Whitman, etc.); the epic form derives from the wish to narrate in a memorable fashion and an artistic manner.

If we move to Italian, on the other hand, the minimal pair "cantare" and "contare"—with the change of vowel in the binomial—gives way, due to its phonetic quality, to another pun based on another rhetorical figure, that is, polysemy: if you allow me to play with words, in Italian the verb "contare" does not mean "recount," but instead "contare" as "to number" and "to count," that is "to be of value" = "essere importante," "avere un valore," "avere autorità," and this can also be interpreted as "to have a voice," which juxtaposes with "cantar," perfectly in keeping with the very essence of poetry translation: to find a voice which sings and (re)counts, as much as the one of the original text. Paz maintained that the dominant word in poetry is "voice." Poetry is the "other voice" allowed to mankind, and all the poets, the latter being really "oyen la voz *otra*" (Paz 1990, 131).

So here we are in the face of an accumulation of voices and otherness: the "other voice" which poetry always represents, and the "other voice" that translating poetry implies. The "other voice," however, which renders poetry from one language to another, prompts an inveterate debate, and the crux of the dilemma translators and translation scholars constantly face in pursuing their profession. When we look for "another voice" in the text at hand, it's an act of trust, "an investment of belief," as Steiner put it (Steiner 1975), placing confidence in the fact that we can pour into the chord progression of another idiom the equivalent poetical harmony created in its pristine form. It's no coincidence that George Steiner calls the first move of his hermeneutic motion "initiative trust" (ibid.).

In referring to the above-mentioned essay on poetry by Octavio Paz—which, by the way, was written as early as 1976—I would like to expand the scope of the adjective "initiative," and in connection with it, also point to the sort of initiatory ritual that runs through Bathanti's compositions, both in the subjective and objective sense. Let me clarify: Bathanti demands that the involved reader comprehend the same initiatory process which he experienced as a child and adolescent: for example, when he elaborated the heroic and mythical male figures of his family, as shown in the poems "Paolo Mio," "Sempre Fidele," "The Headstone," "Prometheus," and "My Father's Hat," just to quote a few examples (in the objective sense). At the same time, he requires that you become, by way of an all-embracing empathy, an initiated participant who shares firsthand the themes of his poetics, almost becoming an actor in the same scene depicted in the poem (in the subjective sense).

The "other voice" Bathanti frequently evokes is, for instance, that of his grandfather, Paolo, who, contrary to his symbolically high status and parental importance—typical of the patriarchal figure of "father" in the Mediterranean vision—never uttered a word in English, and hardly any in Italian either. Perhaps because, in accordance with his authoritative posture, he didn't need to talk; one gesture was enough to let the rest of the family understand what he wanted and what they were supposed to do (the poem from the collection *This Metal*, titled "Paolo Mio" is emblematic in this regard, and the commentary Bathanti himself wrote on this composition is illuminating). However, just because of this lack of words—due to the forced erasure of his primeval language and self-imposed absence of verbal communication—Paolo induces the whole family group to undergo a real loss of identity, which is perceived—and then luckily enough amended—by the aware young grandson, Joseph, who understands he must become Paolo's Hercules and restore the dignity of a different voice. It is young Joseph who, learning from childhood his grandfather's painful alienating experience, embracing his legacy, reverses his family's destiny, and counterbalances the Battiantes' language privation with his powerful poetic lines—lines which re-establish the family's own voice (American and now Italian too), making "contar y cantar" come true.

PRAYER TO HERMES

This is the title of a poem by Robert Creeley ("Prayer to Hermes—for Rafael Lopez-Pedraza," *Later* 1979) included in the *Black Mountain: Poesia & Poetica* anthology that I edited with Annalisa Goldoni in 1987. Here Creeley invokes and celebrates Hermes, god of the doubles ("Hermes, god / of crossed sticks, / crossed existence /

[. . .] Neither one nor two / but a mixture / walks here / in me"). Hermes ("Mercurio" in Italian, hence the day "mercoledì") is also the protecting god of trade, keen on negotiations and "inter-pretium" (hence "interpreter") affairs; Hermes is also the messenger who connects Jupiter in the Olympus with mankind on earth. Being such, under his aegis is translation, a negotiation *par excellence*. In his "Prayer to Hermes" Creeley states "Imagination / is the wonder / of the real" and I believe this credo is convincingly subscribed to by Joseph Bathanti in his poetry, as well. The episodes from his life trigger the poet's imaginative power and become crystallized in luminescent lines radiating in prismatic play.

Talking about the "doubles," one of the highest privileges a translator might ever experience is exactly that of being permitted to "duplicate" the poet's voice in another language. As Bathanti recounted in his preface "Restituted," I first contacted him on the occasion of a special forum devoted to Black Mountain poetry (Morbiducci 2017). We did not meet in person, but corresponded via email. Bathanti kindly agreed to be interviewed, and also consented to giving us four unpublished poems for the so called "L'inedito" section of the journal (the entire interview and all four poems are published in the *RSA Rivista di Studi Americani*, issue #28, 2017, 91-150 and 215-227). Since then, our dialogue on poetry translation has been thriving. Approximately 100 hours spent online followed, from late spring 2021 to date, practically every Wednesday, for almost two years, we would connect on Zoom, and discuss the Italian versions of his poems, in a circle of mutual friendship and esteem, the three of us, Joseph, Darcy, and myself. (By the way, I am not sure if the choice of Wednesday = *Mercoledì* as the day of our meetings was purely a felicitous coincidence with Hermes' day . . .).

It is always an indescribable thrill to translate poems into one's mother tongue, Italian for me. But in the case of rendering Joseph Bathanti's poetry into Italian, the joy, excitement, and passion, really tripled, since, in addition to translating a highly significant and refined American poet—thus allowing the Italian public to be able to appreciate his art—we were all engaged in performing a subtler operation, that is, making the two halves of a whole reunite, 're-echoing' the original

Italian language of his ancestors in his American poems. It was "voice regained," like a religious celebration, a liturgical moment.

Our prayer to Hermes, the god of translation and doubles. "No action is taken without a liturgical frame [. . .] [w]e are constantly reminded that in actual practice the distinction cannot be maintained between superstition and dogma, or between everyday apotropaic gestures and High Mass, or between lived religion and abstract faith," Wittman writes *àpropos* Bathanti's *The 13th Sunday after Pentecost* (2016) (Wittman 2016, 113); then she adds: "[t]he moment becomes liturgical not just via constant references to Catholicism, and its ordering of life, but because the author's sense that the passage of time, the coincidences of personal history and global events, deserve reverence and ritual" (Wittman 2016, 111-112).

Turning to George Steiner's hermeneutic motion: he calls the third step of his sequence "incorporation" or "embodiment" and introduces the metaphor of "sacramental intake" to create a spiritual comparison with the possession or transference that translation arouses when it invests our mind and body. In Bathanti's description of places, circumstances, and daily events, the sacred element is pervasive, even if interspersed in a quite mundane fabric; it's a fusion of elements, a *concordia discors* felicitously achieved. Bathanti combines the rituals at church with the working class shifts in the furnace, the High Mass ceremony with the baseball playground, the sober and silent visit to the cemetery with the sonorous forays into the Hollow. Therefore, I would not say that his Catholic upbringing is the chief element to stand out in his texts. It is certainly always in the background, framing his whole family life, and also the existence of his neighbours, yet the sense of exuberance springing from these quotidian experiences brings to the poetical texture all their nuances of joy, fear, sorrow, hope, and also delusion.

Finally, Steiner rounds up his hermeneutic motion with the fourth move, which is called "restitution" or "compensation," the stage at which the original poem is not only rendered, but even enhanced in the target language: here the receiving language heightens the power of the original in a sort of mystical fusion, and the balance is restored with an enrichment that comes full circle. We are convinced that Bathanti's poems sound beautiful in Italian. The "other voice" resonates proudly and happily in the world, in order to "contar y cantar," as Paz desired (and Hermes would surely approve).

MULTIPLYING VOICES, SILENCES AND SOUNDS

It all starts from breath and inspiration: Bathanti displays his "distinctive voice," "conversational yet lyrical, ironic yet heartfelt. It is not only a question of form; such versatility is rooted in the unstable nature of memory itself," as Andrea Gazzoni put it (Gazzoni 2015, 239). It would be simplistic, however, and probably devious, to believe that Bathanti's work perpetrates a nostalgia operation while providing a personal account of the vicissitudes of his immigrant family. As Fred Gardaphé shrewdly observes, "[t]he pieces of our personal history that come from such places [East Liberty in Pittsburgh] become the building blocks of personality, and [. . .] that past becomes a playground out of which stories, often better than the histories, are spun" (Gardaphé 2016, v).

Contar y cantar, once again. The orchard, the church, the cemetery, the fields, the furnace, the streets, the school, the bridge, the rib joint, the barber's shop, and so on: they are all the urban and human places which populate Bathanti's world. "Bathanti intersperses his poignant poems of Italian heritage with regular ruminations on what was by mid-century the great American pastime: baseball," Mary Jo Bona points out (Bona 2012, xi). Memories and future perspectives—dare I say dreams?—mingle together in the mind of the young boy observing his landscape, the Italian *basilico* and Locatelli cheese combine with eggplants and fresh tomatoes, and then mix with the whiskey and beer of the alternative American tradition; the smell of the dough emanates and blends with the poisoning vapours exhaling from the steel factory. As Bona put it, "The ordinary harshness of everyday life is evinced in *This Metal*, especially in those poems detailing the lives of working-class men. Such poems recall the work of his father and neighborhood men, those mill workers who also suffer silently from accidents, steel strikes, and ill health" (Bona 2012, xii), and the scary image of the weird woman living isolated in the outskirts of town overlaps with the horrific vision of his father's burnt arm.

Everything merges. The silence of the grandfather and father, the distinctive behaviour of the South Italian men ("Silence permeates the life of the old men," as Marina Camboni underscored) (Camboni 2010, 203)—especially when they are in a bad mood, or in a sort of worried temper, I would add—alternates with the constant loquacity of the female members of the family (except his sister Marie, a sort of mysterious and intriguing personality). The call of the huckster in the streets selling silk stockings and dirt-cheap cigarettes overlaps with the priest's liturgical celebration of the Sunday mass at church, the betting in the bars mixes with the barber's gossip, and the cry of the fake suicidal guy on the bridge is shut out by the children's merry laughter in the fields. Like a medieval pageant, the genuine life of the people living there, where Joseph grew up, takes the stage.

Marina Camboni adds, "There is a medieval sense of doom that runs through Bathanti's poems, where sin and death inform the archaeological strata of the poetic persona's memory, together with the rituals and imagination of a boy's Catholic upbringing," and evokes the pictorial fresco that Bathanti's synaesthetic images create in the text (Camboni 2010, 203).

More than Renaissance paintings, in Bathanti's poems, I envision a hallmark of Neo-realism movies (how not to think of *Sciuscià* in the poem describing the barber's shop?), in a complex frame of black-and-white pictures portraying relatives and neighbours, as in the poem of Bathanti's parents' wedding ("From the Photograph of the Church Steps: September 3, 1947"). There is a strong social consciousness and commitment surfacing in these poems, and the private themes intertwine with the public sense of belonging to a community that is a group of outcasts and emarginated people, perhaps, but still a community, resounding with their voices in poetry.

CONCORDIA DISCORS AND REDUCTIO AD UNUM

My interpretation of Bathanti's poetry is that of a noble and superior form of (successful) endeavour to embrace all mankind, or at least, that portion of humanity he is able to circumscribe. Bathanti is inclusive, *ante litteram*—let's say universal? Just by virtue of his idiosyncratic vision, he is able to encompass all walks of life, all trades, all types of personalities. He can see it all, he is a prophet (not Tiresias, because he can observe attentively what surrounds him physically in addition to mentally); as a prophet, he has premonitory dreams, perceives anguish, experiences collapses, falls. "The world is too much with" this young boy, generous and perceptive, insightful and impressionable. We are by his side, as translators, and hold him by the hand in his initiatory discoveries. It is not easy to combine opposites, especially at a young age, but in his maturity Bathanti's poetics is capable of including every aspect of life, and all opposites reconcile. *Concordia discors* is his goal, a superior form of harmony and sympathy encircling, understanding, and bearing all of the suffering and palpitations in the world. This might appear very Christian-like, but it can also be very philanthropic, too. The notion of *felix culpa*, for example, is transferred as well, into a worldly dimension, sending messages of collective and private redemption from life's injustices.

Bathanti is a poet and writer who believes in Leopardi's "umane sorti e progressive," and invites his readers and interlocutors to adopt an optimistic view of the world's evils. Even his ironical bitterness in the face of the harshness of life is never destructive. The boundary between cynicism and humour is never crossed. Bathanti's artistic feat is to make every experience converge in a balanced harmony, and he succeeds.

As translators in Italian we hope to have conveyed the same elegant and empathic sense of balance through his "other voice."

MARINA MORBIDUCCI
Rome
February 22, 2023
Ash Wednesday

WORKS CITED

Bathanti, J. (2010) *Restoring Sacred Art*, Star Cloud Press, Scottsdale, AZ.

_____ (2013) *Concertina*, Mercer University Press, Macon, GA.

_____ (2016) *The 13th Sunday after Pentecost*, Louisiana State University Press, Baton Rouge, LA.

_____ (2022) *Light at the Seam*, Louisiana State University Press (Baton Rouge, LA), 2022.

Bona, M. J. (2012) "Introduction" to Joseph Bathanti, *This Metal*, Press 53, Winston-Salem, NC, xi-xvi.

Camboni, M. (2013) "Review," Joseph Bathanti, *Restoring Sacred Art*, in *Italian Americana*, Vol. 31, No. 2, Summer 2013, 203-206.

Creeley, R. (1979) *Later*, New Directions, New York.

Gazzoni, A. (2015) "A Major Voice in Italian-American Literature and the Art of Writing from Memory," *Italian Americana*, 3 (2), 239-242.

Gardaphé, F. (2016) "Foreword" to Joseph Bathanti, *East Liberty*, University of South Carolina Press, Columbia, SC, v-ix.

Goldoni, A. and Morbiducci, M. (1987) (Eds) *Black Mountain: Poesia & Poetica*, La Goliardica, Roma.

Morbiducci, M. (2017) "Forum: Black Mountain College. Revisiting Projections, 60 Years After," *RSAJournal (Rivista di Studi Americani, Journal of AISNA / Italian Association of North American Studies)* 28/2017, 91-150.

Morbiducci, M. (2017) "L'inedito," "Interview with Joseph Bathanti," *RSAJournal (Rivista di Studi Americani, Journal of AISNA / Italian Association of North Amercian Studies)* 28/2017, 215-227.

Paz, O. (1990) *La otra voz*, Seix Barral, Barcelona.

Steiner, G. (1975) *After Babel*, OUP, Oxford.

Wittman, L. (2018), "Review" of Joseph Bathanti's *The 13th Sunday after Pentecost, Italian Americana*, Vol. XXXVI, No. 1, Winter 2018, 111-113.

A Tour of Bathanti Country

The 21st century affords wholly new opportunities for one and all, such as the revision of translated poems during Zoom meetings, and with the privilege of having the poet himself on hand, from the other side of the ocean. A particularly generous poet, willing to meet weekly, with few exceptions, for going on two years now, squeezing us into his lunch hour, between classes, in North Carolina, while in Rome it is just before dinner, and frankly, we haven't even thought about that yet. And a rather odd triangle, I would imagine, presented itself, comprised of said poet, Joseph Bathanti; the sophisticated, *italianissima* translator, Marina Morbiducci, professor of Translation Studies and Italy's expert on Gertrude Stein—and me: the go-between. An American, long-time expat, teacher and translator herself, who looks back on the New World with wonder and yearning, just as the poet's grandfather, a key figure in these poems, fixed his mind's eye on the Old.

The lion's share of this labor of love, *Sempre Fidele and Other Poems*, has been done by the time the Zoom call starts: Joseph Bathanti has written most of the poems even decades before, and Marina Morbiducci has recently translated them, one by one, week by week, in the privacy of her own home, or other workspace. I log on as a fresh pair of eyes, a third intelligence brought to bear on this live revision, so to speak: querying the poet, in English, on his references to American culture and geography and discussing, in Italian, the Italian equivalents with the translator. The latter, *italianissima*, is more at home with the poems' myriad nods to Catholicism, while my own Protestant Irish-American mother outweighed my Italian-American, lapsed Catholic father, and I myself am at sea. The former—Italian-American, honorary North Carolinian, poet laureate and by now a perfect southern gentleman, in my fantasy—lets the scraps of current Italian dialogue wash over him, patiently, politely, and even curiously—the language of his ancestors that he soaked up in childhood little sounding, perhaps, like the vernacular of Rome sixty-odd years later.

Which brings us to the challenges of translating mid-20th-century Italian terms, or Italian-American dialect, into standard 21st-century

Italian, and not only: when my calico kitten jumped on my head, mid-Zoom, I taught the poet the meaning of her name, Mizzica. He loved the sound, shouting "Mizzica!" with an enormous smile. I explained it's sort of Sicilian for 'wow.' He has asked after her ever since.

Ironic as this may sound, many Italian terms often italicized in the original poems need to be tossed and replaced in the Italian versions in 2023. What Bathanti calls *Romas* will have to be *pomodori*, or tomatoes. Possibly: San Marzano. *Gavone* will not register on this side of the pond I am on: I google it and find it to be Italian-American dialect for 'boor', 'one with crude manners', or: 'someone who eats a lot'. But Americans can relax: they will be familiar with the term from *The Sopranos*. And we'll leave it, a perfect match for the cultural setting of these poems. Today's Romans, cut off in traffic, or on a long line at the Poste, or whatnot, hurl a clearly-related *cafone* at the offender.

American terms also get a workover in this our labor of love. A bowtie morphs into a *farfallina* (little butterfly), a tuxedo into the enigmatic *frac*; a delicatessen (of German origin) winds up Lost in Translation, becoming a generic 'grocery store'; and as for a finger bowl: we wave the white flag and spell it out: *ciotole d'acqua per pulirsi le dita*. Oh, how the genius and economy of the English language do shine in its compound nouns! To return to negative personality types, an 'operator' triggers a key Italian archetype, the *furbo*, or, even better, *il furbacchione*. Other juicy examples abound in the examination of select poems from this bilingual collection that follows (the collection draws on a larger body of poems that got the 'Zoom treatment' starting in July 2021).

Thematically, we will be looking at American geography, then at scattered appeals to that 'paradise lost', the Italy the poet's grandfather left behind in the early years of the last century. And at American culture, largely that of the 1950s and '60s, with a few leaps forward to more recent decades. What Italian readers will see is their Ur-Italian culture *superimposed* on an American landscape in the first half of the booming 20th century, dubbed 'the American century', of late; it's a culture filtered through the memories of a child, now a man pushing seventy. And this treasure trove is now 're-translated' into Italian, and well into the 21st century, landing in an Italy that arguably bears little resemblance to its previous iterations before, during, and after the world wars.

The Italian culture spilling out of the poems will then be examined and subdivided roughly into family, food, and a small group I call 'Italian characters', in the sense of eccentrics. Food being a corollary of the Italian family, the last major theme is the underlying thread of Catholicism, and not so underlying, at that. This is the religion that, sixty, seventy, eighty years ago, dictated the daily and weekly rituals of the transplanted Italians; and the poet's own profound religious feeling transcends ritual and emanates from his work.

The American landscape is rough and raw (all stereotypes apply) and as exotic to present-day Italian readers as it is to me, reared in the canyons of Manhattan: the setting is Pittsburgh, Pennsylvania. Let us locate it on a map: on the western end of the state, facing Ohio and roads west; the eastern Great Lakes to the north, West Virginia to the south; and the city lies just west of the Appalachian Mountains—more specifically the Alleghenies. Pittsburgh, steel capital of America until 1980 or so, is shaped by two rivers, the Allegheny and the Monongahela, which meet there to form the Ohio River that will eventually flow into the Mississippi. Pittsburgh: a gateway, unquestionably. In his very recent poem, "Limbo," Bathanti summons up Carl Galie's photograph *Almost Heaven* to describe the vantage point:

> an endless sweep of the ancient
> *un'infinita distesa dell'inveterata catena*
> Appalachian chain, just the peaks,
> *dei monti Appalachi, proprio le cime,*
> in autumnal brilliance,
> *nella lucentezza autunnale,*
> to their chins in cottony vapor,
> *fino al loro mento in nubi d'ovatta,*

Italian readers and Manhattanites alike thrill to the idea of the frontier, and the Appalachians were an early frontier. Let us now descend into the nit and grit of the city itself, where the poet was raised. A city of hills, hollows, and river bridges, it is a protagonist in the story of his life in every way. In the poem "Lincoln Avenue," tired nurses and stonecutters—a nice cross-section of the population in East Liberty, the poet's home turf—wait "for the last trolley up Cemetery Hill" after work. Yet there is relief up on the hill, though the trolley labors mightily to get there:

> Steel wheels on steel rails rutted
> > *Ruote d'acciaio su binari d'acciaio*
> in gray ten-pound cobbles screeched
> > *incastonati tra sanpietrini da cinque chili stridevano*
> and sparked as streetcars
> > *e facevano scintille mentre i tram*
> freighted straphangers to rib joints
> > *trasportavano passeggeri appesi alle maniglie*
> and storefront clubs on the Hill
> > *diretti alle locande e ai bar sulla collina*

Those hard-edged consonants and cacophonic verbs—we can hear the poet's scratchy wheels and gears all the way over here in Rome, in 2023—yield to longer, softer vowel-filled solutions in Italian. And while American readers know from straphangers and rib joints, neither has a handy translation in Italian, there being no 'joints' to taste 'ribs' in, and no bus passengers dignified, or mortified, by any other name. In addition, the 'cobbles' here are 'Romanized' into *sanpietrini* ('little St. Peter's', the name for them in Rome alone).

In "Larimer Avenue," the cityscape is instantly recognizable to an American, at least to those familiar with older American cities on the Eastern Seaboard or in the Midwest: "where houses squat in rows" and "Old men think on porch gliders." Italian buildings in cities are taller; how to convey those low-slung fronts plastered over hills and dales? The image doesn't spring to an Italian mind, and the translation remains literal. And those porch gliders? The oldsters 'swing' (*si dondolano*) on their verandas (*loggetta*). The poet and his family, in their '63 Belair, "cross the Meadow Street Bridge into the gut of ancestry," presumably the "Little Italy" of Pittsburgh.

'Ancestry' proves to be a difficult concept to translate; I've almost never heard it in conversation among my forward-looking Italian friends, attracted to what glistens—and that is the present. They go regional at best—Tuscan, Venetian, Sicilian—while roots remain a canonical American preoccupation. The translator puts *Le viscere* [guts] *della progenie* [progenie].

In the poem "The Hollow," we get an even better feel for the territory. The bridge is again the Meadow Street Bridge, which appears to span a chasm: the Hollow. (The *italianissima* translator wonderfully dubs it *Lo Sprofondo*.) "The old Italian people," the poet writes, called it *Bassa la Vallone*: something like the 'bottom of the big valley'. What we care about is what's there and where our poet romped, as a child: 'his' woods, "a swath of sumac / and crabapples stuck to the shoulder / of Negley Run," where he went and huddled, "skinning / a bow and arrows with my first knife," surely a *novello* Huckleberry Finn, our Italian readers will enthuse. Courageous, as well: a child-eating monster, Spacaluccio, is rumored to live under the bridge. The poet looks back:

> What was I doing there—drawn incessantly
> *Che ci facevo là—trascinato senza tregua*
> deeper into the white gleaming green,
> *sempre più giù nello splendente verde,*
> drinking water from a stone,
> *mentre bevevo acqua dalla pietra,*
> not getting in from the rain nor making a sound,
> *senza ripararmi dalla pioggia né emettere un rumore,*
> eating only the tiny apples
> *mangiando solo quelle melette*
> that tasted so much of a foreign tongue?
> *che sapevano tanto di lingua straniera?*

Depths, heights, and now, curiously, language creeps in. The poet's father—not his grandfather, this time—puts in a dramatic appearance high over the steelworks in Pittsburgh in the poem "This Metal":

> This is my father's country.
> *Questa la terra di mio padre.*
> High above Andrew Carnegie's first blast
> *Lassù in alto sulle prime fornaci di Carnegie,*
> furnaces, he swung on boom
> *lui è stato sospeso*
> cranes for forty years with thirty
> *sulle gru per quarant'anni con trenta libbre*

> pounds of steel on his hips.
> > *d'attrezzi d'acciaio sui fianchi.*
> He saw men die on the open hearth.
> > *Vide uomini morire nelle fornaci a cielo aperto.*

Note that while it was feasible in Italian to have old men 'swing' on their porch gliders in "Larimer Avenue," swinging dangerously on boom cranes is another matter entirely; in Italian the poet's father is 'suspended' in air on his *gru* (the bird as well as the boom crane). In any case, we are shown a Pittsburgh of dizzying heights and wild lows.

Our tour of the contours of Pittsburgh and western Pennsylvania ends on a poignant yet very near comical note. We learn in "Paolo Mio" that the poet's grandfather buried his wife "out of country / in a hill filled with Lutherans / and never returned." Bathanti explained why during a Zoom meeting: Paolo believed that St. Peter's Cemetery was Catholic, and learned too late that it wasn't. That hill "filled with Lutherans" resonates more with Americans than Italians, who see few of them and have no hills packed with them—unless we count the American war cemeteries in places like Anzio, or the Protestant Cemetery in Rome where Keats lies, his name "writ in Water," sites where one might run a better chance. It's in "Memento Mori," a section of the poem "Sempre Fidele," that the idea is fleshed out somewhat, as we follow the poet as a child as he and his sister accompany his father to tend to the grave of his misplaced grandmother:

> helping our father find
> > *mentre aiutiamo nostro padre a rintracciare*
> his mother's moiety of feudal dirt;
> > *l'atavico pezzo di terra di sua madre;*
> her cantle of America, here in this cemetery
> > *la sua porzione d'America, qui in questo cimitero*
> by mistake, alone among Lutherans;
> > *per errore, unica tra le tombe luterane;*
> choked by catbrier and morning glory.
> > *soffocate dal rampicante e le campanule.*

The lovely-sounding words 'moiety' and 'cantle' are sacrificed here to the more pedestrian *pezzo* and *porzione*, while 'feudal' won't do—too history-specific, too despotic in Italian—and we fall back on the rather glamorous *atavico*, while English scores another point with its startling 'morning glory' that shatters the funereal air.

Cemetery or not, this land is our land: the poet muses that "We've inherited this land, / his father's venial blunder." In the same poem, the child's attention turns, once again, to the horizon, the Americans' eternal attraction to that punch-packing myth, its frontier (while the emigrants' attention, before leaving, was drawn west from Italy to another horizon: coastal America as a vision, a landfall):

> We watch the Allegheny
> > *Vediamo il fiume Allegheny*
> pushing west toward the equinox,
> > *spingersi a ovest verso l'equinozio,*
> its surrounding slopes mauled by snow.
> > *i suoi declivi circostanti sfigurati dalla neve.*

For there to be so much snow on the slopes, it must be the spring equinox in March. It must be March, for the poet to place the equinox to the west, a 'move' that struck me, as I've always imagined the equinox as a belt, somewhere south of us, but north of the equator—as I sheepishly realized, reading the line. The snow 'disfigures' the slopes in Italian: the mauling animal has gone out of the metaphor.

What of Italy, paradise lost? Nostalgia becomes more acute in old age, and in another section of the poem "Sempre Fidele," "Litany," the poet's grandfather Paolo Battiante (even the name was changed on Ellis Island, the poet has told us) recalls "the smell of olive / blossoms / spreading the hills of Foggia." He was born in Manfredonia in 1877, and came to America at age thirty, no younger. Nostalgia bears with it anger: his grandfather does not wish, the poet tells us in "Litany," "to die in this hemisphere." "A man who leaves his country," the poet opines in the same section, "is forever whelped by illusion, / never knowing whenness from destiny." Illusion moves people around the globe. Is *that* destiny, or else 'whenness': meaning occasion, I wonder? Seizing the day? The translator puts *il singolo attimo*, 'each second'. I find the dry definition 'existence at a particular point in time.'

Had Paolo stayed in Italy? In "Midnight," another section of "Sempre Fidele," the poet claims, "In *Italia* / he would have been a baron"—the Italian version opts for *un blasonato*, someone with a coat of arms, a noble—"and I, the apple of his only eye / would cross the Apennines / to the Mediterranean." More mountains, more travel, more opportunity for the man's son. But on the Italian side, the Apennines are not planted in a vast continent; they are squeezed between seas with changing names: the Tyrrhenian, the Ionian, the Adriatic. The descent from the heights ends fast, down on that wine-dark sea out of which the emigrants of yore wended on their ships, to cross the steely Atlantic, as the poet imagines in "A Better Life":

> A thousand kilometers from Apulia,
> > *A mille chilometri dalla Puglia,*
> the sea is an oracle
> > *il mare è un oracolo*
> coiling at the gunwales:
> > *che s'attorciglia sulla trinca della nave:*

His grandfather claims he had lost an eye "on his last ride with Garibaldi"; Garibaldi died when he was five years old—no matter. In the poem his lost eye "swills in a trench / along the Gulf of Taranto." Paolo himself sails "to America with trowel / and hammer, one eye, no voice." In America, the grandfather prophesizes in "A Better Life," he will "remain alone" and "live unacquainted / even with the ghosts who needle me." An expat's lot, indeed! And indeed, the grandfather lashes out, in closing:

> God did not prepare me for this bitch country.
> > *Dio non mi ha preparato per questo paese maledetto.*
> My hand is against it.
> > *La mia mano lo rigetta.*
> Let my blood make peace.
> > *Ci faccia pace la mia progenie.*

'Bitch' becomes 'cursed' in Italian; anything else would be too long for the line. We've seen *progenie* already; it is a fancy and prettier word for blood, or offspring. *Sangue* (blood) would have suggested violence, or death of the speaker, or sacrifice on this order, and not the rich legacy of one's descendants, or bloodline (*sangue del mio sangue*, however, happens to be a folksier term for that).

No time for such gloomy observations as Paolo's when you're a young man swinging on boom cranes, with a young wife and children to feed. The poet's father is a real American. Second-generation Italian. And, as the poems show, he has all the trappings, starting with a series of automobiles (the '56 Plymouth in "Memento Mori," the '63 Belair in "Larimer Avenue"), while many years earlier, the poet's mother is a young girl "leaning cockily on the fender of a two-toned roadster, with a rumble seat" in 1937; the poet summons her and her vehicle from an old photograph in "Mendicant on a Bridge."

The look the women have, as the poet remembers from his childhood, screams 1950s America: "The women, in sleeveless summer dresses, / fountains of hair scarved at their crowns," in the poem "The Huckster"; the huckster himself has silk stockings to sell. The poet's mother is like something out of *Mad Men* as she primps and preens for High Mass on Sunday, her son watching from the four-poster bed in the poem "High Mass," as his mother "in a slip, at her vanity," [. . .]:

> Around her neck fastened pearls,
>   *Attorno al collo chiudeva un giro di perle,*
> dipped each ear to earring,
>   *inclinando la testa, affondava nei lobi gli orecchini,*
> slipped into her dress and called,
>   *scivolava dentro il vestito e poi chiamava il nome di*
> Joe, my father's name—to zip it.
>   *mio padre,* Joe, *che le tirasse su la zip.*

Joe, "dark, clean-shaven," a double for Don Draper, obliges. Yet the translator cannot oblige us when it comes to the lovely, economical dipping of each ear to earring; the literal translation of the Italian becomes: "tilting her head, she sinks the earrings in her lobes." No matter. 'Zip' is no verb in Italian: you pull up the *zip*, or *lampo*.

All this finery on the Sundays when the poet's father was "on strike from steel," in the same poem, yet he sweated his shifts, and the poet catches them in the reflection in the mirror when he's a boy on the barber's seat in "The Headstone": "a dismissed Peabody shift / strolling toward Vento's Pizza." The barber makes dirty jokes about women and "calls them *broads*." Lost in translation! The translator finally hits the nail on the head with an appropriately retro *femmine*. Another quintessential American figure is present at the barbershop, but no worries: we have a word for him in Italian, which looks Italian but sounds just like the original. "Frankie, the Shine, plops / on a stack of *Playboys*, writing numbers." That would be the shoeshine, or the *sciuscià*. Note the American touch of those *Playboys*, in their 'glory' days, readership-wise.

Kids play "Indian-ball in the schoolyard" in "Larimer Avenue" (the translator opts for 'baseball'); in Stoebner Alley in the same poem, the ground is "trashed with old soldiers— / Manischewitz, Wild Irish Rose." The poet has to tell the *italianissima* translator, and remind the long-time expat, that old soldiers are empty bottles, which is what they become in Italian. No Italian match for the evocative idiom concerning the custom of tossing empty bottles in the street, it seems. No Italian custom either, it follows?

Yet all is not well in East Liberty, a neighborhood contested by the Italian immigrants and the native Blacks. The poet's father, in "Turns," "drove his black comrades / to the mill when they shared turns." "The blacks who walked here," notes the poet in the same poem, "were daygirls and yardmen / who never lifted their eyes from the street," but now:

> The city on fire, King was dead.
>   *La città in fiamme, King era morto.*
> Surrounded by what had been built by slave labor,
>   *Circondato da edifici costruiti dalla fatica di schiavi,*
> we smelled smoke across the river.
>   *sentimmo odor di fumo venire da oltre il fiume.*

An American instantly gets the reference. The *italianissima* translator is told that not just any king is dead, but MLK. It's now 1968, in the poem "Turns." Five years earlier, in "The Death of East Liberty," "The Catholic had been assassinated, / his Frontier swept away / by glass and brick dust." Americans, but only Italians who are history buffs, seize on the reference instantly. Be it JFK in Dallas or *West Side Story* filmed in the wreckage of Hell's Kitchen, urban renewal has now come to East Liberty, Pittsburgh. "The wrecking ball emptied the sky like an atom bomb," and "Half the voters could not speak English / to save their homes." They were given "five grand" to move, but, the poet cautions, "demolition had crept into the bloodline," and "Italians went to their graves without speaking, / wholly terrified of America."

Those bucolic woods in the Hollow under the bridge, where the poet played? They were "wedged between / cliffs of mixed hungers: black and immigrant," he explains in "The Hollow." The two groups "fought with rocks and sticks, / and screamed across the abyss at each other." It's the same 'hood' that the poet as a boy had observed more happily from his earliest youth, in "Lincoln Avenue":

> From our Lincoln duplex, crosscut
>   *Dalla nostra palazzina bifamiliare,*
> by black mortuaries and African temples,
>   *intersecata da camere mortuarie e templi africani,*
> I watched spectacular wakes.
>   *osservavo spettacolari veglie.*

'Duplex,' in passing, meant not the two-storey high-end apartment a Manhattanite instantly calls to mind, but, again, as the poet explained to us on Zoom, the smallest of single houses split between two families (one upstairs, one downstairs). The translator renders it as such. We are back to a quintessentially American building type and 'look'. As for "black mortuaries" and "African temples": the Italian translator pauses visibly, to absorb the fact that there were funeral parlors for Blacks and others for Italians, as there were churches for Blacks and others for others.

Italian culture is threaded into this fantastical tapestry, this urban fabric. American readers are familiar with the cast of characters and the customs seen here from the eating places and the festivals, films, novels, and more recently TV series that hold up a mirror to Italian-American culture. They will recognize the poet's mother and other female figures, whether dressing up or home cooking: his dapper father; his teenage sister lost in a book; and even his moody grandfather, the patriarch. An actual 'Godfather' appears, in the Catholic sense of the term, in "Saint Marie Street"; joining the poet's father and staring outside from a screen door, as they "pour / shots and beers and tell a joke— / the kind, twenty years ago, / I was too young to laugh at."

"From the Photograph of the Church Steps: September 3, 1947" captures the cheerful chaos of a wedding at the moment the bride (the poet's mother), the groom and the guests spill out of the church. The bride is "wise-cracking" to the groom. The best man is "dreadfully handsome," and "despised" by the bride: "an operator, a *gavone*" ("*un furbacchione, un gavone,*" in the Italian version). An unidentified man, his back to the camera, is also deftly drawn by the poet, with his cinematic eye: "He rushes madly / back into Our Lady's."

But it is the poet's grandfather who steals the scene, again and again. We first meet him in "Paolo Mio," now dead and "boxed," but evoked in a very live version, dancing "the Tarantella / in Sunday shirt and gold watch"; brooding "over Chianti and fierce Parodis"; and drunkenly "invoking *Jesu* and Garibaldi in one breath." In a nice touch, the scarecrow in the garden "wears his fedora." For all that, we learn elsewhere that, when sober, Paolo is a man of few words. Practically none. His son, the poet's father, as well: "I can't remember a single sentence passed between them," the poet admits in "The Headstone." The poem "Silence" features an epigraph from Cesare Pavese's *South Seas*:

> Silence is a family trait.
> Some ancestor of ours must have been a solitary man—
> a great man surrounded by halfwits, or a poor, crazy fool—
> to teach his descendants such silence.

And Bathanti himself adds, in "The Headstone":

> Yet I feel the pall of silence stealing over me.
> *Eppure sento il peso incombente del silenzio.*
> My grandfather refused to speak English.
> *Mio nonno ha sempre rifiutato di parlare inglese.*
> We knew when he lifted his hand,
> *Quando sollevava la mano gli altri capivano*

he was finished.
che aveva finito.

Italian readers will smile at this, and at the host of supporting and very Italian characters that peoples the poet's imagination. Old man Labriola sells olives out of barrels in "Larimer Avenue," the avenue "where every John thinks he's a gangster." Labriola "sidles warily onto the sidewalk, / checks his flanks as if expecting ambush" and "suspiciously / lugs hanging tuns of provolone and salami / back into his musty store." And that best man in the wedding picture from 1947? Silvio Vento: like the wind, his last name, he would disappear and reappear twenty years later, "then disappear again to his hideout in Florida." And what of the Huckster in the poem of the same name? "He looked like Paladin, Caravaggio," the poet muses, with "a cruel face, filthy with stubble, / rakish silent movie mustache," and is "dressed like an Abruzzi peasant, / white kerchief tied at his neck," "his every move exquisitely choreographed, / as if a wizard, spinning, out of thin air, / apricots, nectarines, peaches."

How do the female characters fare? Graziella, in the poem of the same name, has an evil eye, or so the poet as a child believes (we lose these fine three 'ings' below in the Italian version):

> When she appeared, hair netted
> *Quando lei appariva, con i capelli raccolti nella retina*
> like a black carapace, soothsaying,
> *come un carapace nero, divinatorio,*
> penance-hawking,
> *che intimava pentimento,*
> our games fell to her mourning:
> *i nostri giochi si interrompevano al suo lutto:*

Maria Roselina is the name of the poet's mother, seen in the poem of the same name in her old age, ailing, yet rallying to cook yet another Italian meal, *tagliatelle*, with vegetables from the garden. There are loaves of a curious bread, *Siciliano*, and her husband is grating the *Pecorino* (which I knew as a child as *Romano*), while the table is set with china for the two courses, summoned here in Italian, "for *primi, secondo.*" The scene is what the poet so aptly calls "the unhurried, comforting office of the table," yet his mother, standing over "the large silver pot / we have worshipped all our lives," here achieves the status of a divinity, or a sybil (the water with the pasta, in fact, "roils like an oracle"):

> Prophetically,
>   *Profeticamente,*
> she elevates the wooden spoon.
>   *eleva il mestolo di legno.*
> Behind her, columns of steam
>   *Dietro di lei, colonne di vapore*
> rise and roost
>   *s'alzano e posano*
> in her white hair
>   *nei suoi capelli bianchi*
> like little statues.
>   *come simulacri.*

In "Eggplant," the poet's mother is seen pressing the rounds "to draw out the bitter water" with her tailor father's "heart-shaped iron." In "Braciole," she goes to work on flank steak with the aim of cooking up meat "scrolls," or *involtini*, in the Italian version, and readers are treated to Bathanti's usual delectable catalog of ingredients. She, too, uses a special heirloom to hammer the meat finely: "With the cast iron claw / hammer—burnished / silver in endless / bouts of fire, forged / in Manfredonia, Puglia, / by my blacksmith / grandfather, Paolo / Battiante." The rolls are dropped into the majesty of the sauce "to roil / the rest of our lives. Amen." At this potent image of the meat rolls in the sauce, the poet reverently ends on a prayer. Italian readers will nod, knowingly.

    The Catholic faith is never far from the surface in Bathanti's poems and arranges the calendar of the Italian-American lives in the New World. Even in Rome today, a secular city despite the presence of the Pope, church attendance may have dwindled to almost nothing, but the rites of passage are fully booked: baptisms, confirmation, weddings, funerals. The poet as a child duly hits every milestone; a few are in this collection. The poem "Confirmation" takes us through this sacrament, as the poet bones up on every aspect of the faith, even the "stational churches in Rome" (just *basiliche* in the Italian version), only for the

Bishop to administer nothing but "a dry slap and palsied stamp of chrism." Indeed, the Italian for the rite is *cresima*, also the translator's title for the poem.

The poet as a pre-teen, at this event, "in the home movies, is a sweet boy / in a red blazer"; in reality, he spent most of it thinking of the girls in his class, "their long straight hair and consecrated bodies." Sexuality is dawning. In "Kyrie," we find him marched to the blackboard, in his strict Catholic school, sentenced to writing over and over, in "penitent script," "*I am cursed a sinful boy*"; more corporal punishments are alluded to. The poem's portrait of a nun is titillating:

> I've had truck with the devil,
> *Ho fatto un patto col diavolo, lei mi dice,*
> she says, raven-eyed, gorgeous:
> *i suoi occhi neri come la pece, bellissima:*
> wimple and jackboot oxfords,
> *con soggolo e scarpe pesanti,*
> black hose, big rosary.
> *calze nere, un imponente rosario.*

The marvelously English noun 'truck' is reduced to a more conventional 'pact' in Italian, and while "raven-haired" might easily become *capelli corvini*, for the lovely "raven-eyed," *occhi corvini* won't cut it; they come out *come la pece*, or pitch-black. The poet offsets these erotic musings by having another slice of urban americana enter stage-right, as it were, hearing outside "the drunks on Flavel Street, / hailing me with empty pints / against the black iron grate."

In "The Feast of the Assumption, 1920," a section of the poem "Sempre Fidele," American readers will recognize the typical Italian-American procession down the streets: "The Papists are at their sorcery in the streets," the poet notes impishly. We see "Our Lady's / blue banner / tacked with dollar bills," the dollar-bill part of which the *italianissima* translator struggled mightily to render, but we New Yorkers have seen them tacked all our lives. A jarring upstairs scene is introduced by the poet to spoil the party: "Above them, in a small room, / a woman is dead to childbirth." Her body is carried into "the dancing streets."

Life and death, so exuberantly underscored in a Catholic childhood, gives way to innocence restored in "Son of a Priest," which the poet imagines himself to be as he accompanies his father on a janitor stint at Saints Peter and Paul (during another strike at the plant). As his father dusts and swabs, the child has the run of the church, tabernacle, sacristy cabinets, and altar ("Every sacred object, I touched. / I washed my face in holy water, / sipped it.").

Exhausted from his labors, the poet as a child recalls: "I slunk into Saint Joseph's Chapel, / where I was baptized, / and fell asleep / on its single red-cushioned pew." His trustfulness is perhaps the fountainhead of faith. And Bathanti is a man of faith. Just look at his description of the statue of the Virgin Mary in the poem "Mayday": "The pearl crown sits on its satin pillow / awaiting the coronation. The Madonna / smiles, the serpent wrapped around her / porcelain foot, impaled heart flaming / on the blue bodice."

And the poet's typical American note that follows is a note of mercy: "In the alley, a couple hobos lean / over a salamander." And that was no lizard, mind: we were told it's a fire lit in a barrel on the street for warmth. The translator, reviving, gives us *un falò in un bidone*. The children in this poem, though, don't feel the cold. It's a blizzard in May in Pittsburgh, with a note of cosmic innocence added: "Kids sled into the Hollow's / white cup. Beneath them, / the earth curves."

The truth is, while the poet's imagination expertly captures his countrymen and his family, he takes frequent flights in the direction of the divine. In the poem "Limbo," the tricky dogma of a limbo for infants takes the form of that "endless sweep of the ancient / Appalachian chain, just the peaks," encountered earlier in this essay, where "unbaptized babies" are "not in pain / happy at this altitude." In "Light at the Seam," up on Pine Mountain, Bell County, Kentucky, the poet summons up "Jesus, flanked by Moses / and Elijah, transfigured, / *up into a high mountain / apart*." The reference to Matthew 17: 1-25 is just as familiar to Italians. Then Bathanti swoops down, and not for the first time, to consider ordinary mortals, this time deep in the bowels of the earth: "Deep within, / miners suspire, / shake light at the seam." Given Jesus, Moses, and Elijah high above them, this strikes me as the most spiritual line of poetry in the collection, and also the toughest line to translate: "*Giù in profondità / i minatori prendono fiato, / puntano la luce alla vena*." The lights on the miners' bobbing helmets splash across the walls of the cave (Plato's?), searching for the seam (*vena mineraria* in Italian): the vein of 'this metal' (title of another poem here), the pulse of the divine.

It comes as a shock, then, when we encounter the poet decades later than the main action, as a father of young children himself in "Aunt Nina in Mid-Air," or waiting for his elderly father as he is stripped down by (homeland) security, in our budding new century, coming off a flight in "Domenico Giuseppe." As a young man, Bathanti has escaped his landlocked childhood and started traveling, never severing that familial bond, sending his mother letters "from desperate reaches above the Atlantic" in "Mendicant on a Bridge"—the word 'reaches' deliberately vague, hard to translate: our translator goes with the lovely *sponde*. "She twirls the globe to find me— / never there. The world turns me / sadly over like a boy on a spit." Bathanti involves her at every stop along the way: "We travel together in these letters: / to the Pacific, the Aegean; / any sea; a new conception, / a more harrowing gestation." He remembers her at his age, in the photo by the roadster on a bridge in 1937, "a bridge still standing / uncrashed into the Hollow." Crashed! But still standing for eternity, in these poems.

It's even more startling to find the poet with his grown son in New York City, in the poem "For Frank O'Hara." They have a loft (lost, admittedly, in translation, and usually left in English, but we get a perhaps too high-end *attico*) by Gramercy Park. My own homesickness kicks in here. They go for Indian food in Curry Hill. It's too late to make it to an exhibition, but the colors bleed, in the rain, in the posters for "Bodies: an Exhibition," and in typical Bathanti fashion, those images are dissected accordingly. The poet is worlds away from East Liberty, before or after the wrecking ball, and decades away from the time he was a son only. With just the right consonant clusters, he masterfully captures a visual and cultural motif of the Big Apple: "Bright yellow the queued glistening cabs."

"*I taxi giallo vivo in coda riluccicano*": we've lost the hardness and capsule-like nature of "cabs" and "queued," but we've gained a nice *giallo vivo* and some savvy Italian consonant play in *riluccicano*. In the end, this kind of trade-off is what it's all about, in translation. Conveying meaning is hard enough; conveying culture can be even more daunting.

To conclude, Italian readers will find a lot to like in this collection. It resembles a *gioco di specchi*, a somewhat careworn term in Italian journalism with no real equivalent in English: neither a hall of mirrors nor a mirror game, you could call it the interplay of multiple reflections to produce a pleasing visual effect. Italians will be moved to witness, in these poems, the continuity of their customs and religious feeling juxtaposed, often jarringly, on a seemingly raw, mid-20th century American landscape, cityscape, and streetscape. It's a fabric woven with factories and rows of houses clinging tenaciously to steep hills; vigorous American rivers carving paths more like chasms through the city of Pittsburgh; and socially speaking, long seasons of social unrest and even upheaval; lastly, a 'human capital' with infinite reserves of longing and nostalgia, for youth, for one's battles in the New World, for lost origin stories in the Old (as readers will have guessed by now, I myself largely experience these tides of feeling in reverse). And all of this just a drive away from celestial mountain ranges that form the spine of our Eastern Seaboard but float west, where the poet resides today—and where he found "Almost Heaven" (in the poem "Limbo" here, though the John Denver song is what Americans will hear), and where he converses with the sublime.

DARCY DI MONA
Rome
February 2023

SEMPRE FIDELE

They know where we're going:
across Meadow Street Bridge, into the gut of ancestry.

Loro lo sanno dove stiamo andando:
passando per Meadow Street Bridge, fin dentro le viscere della progenie.

Paolo mio

Con appresso i suoi attrezzi di fabbro ferraio
in una terra giunto che gli negava il fuoco,
piantò i suoi primi semi
e ad ogni primavera gli uccelli

rubavano i suoi frutti, lasciandolo
legnoso e incollerito come un falso profeta,
orbo a un occhio,
l'altro come una biglia di vetro opaco.

Quando sua moglie morì, la fece seppellire
fuori dal Bel Paese sulla collina
piena di Luterani
per non tornarci più.

Nascosto dietro il pergolato di viti,
sentivo la sua rabbia scorrermi dentro.
Già da allora capivo
d'essere il suo Ercole.

Con visione sfocata, vedo
il suo corpo nella bara come fosse vivo
nella stanza sua al buio
dove dormiva solo

mentre ballava la tarantella
con la camicia bianca della festa e l'orologio d'oro,
pensoso col suo Chianti e il feroce Parodi.
Le figlie sue che lui non distingueva

Paolo Mio

Carrying a smith's tools
in a land which would not brook his fire,
he planted seeds,
and each year the birds

took his first fruit, leaving him
to rave woodenly like a false prophet,
one eye blind,
the other like a smoked marble.

When his wife died, he buried her
out of country in a hill
filled with Lutherans
and never returned.

Hiding in the grape arbor,
I felt his anger coursing through me.
Even then I knew
I was his Hercules.

One eye squinted, I see
his now-boxed body alive
in the shuttered room
where he slept alone

and danced the Tarantella
in Sunday shirt and gold watch,
brooded over Chianti and fierce Parodis.
His daughters, whom he could not distinguish

dalle pescivendole mi tiravano via dalla porta.
Ma dopo la sbornia,
tutti lo sentivamo rasposo sciorinare
la sua *compieta* in dialetto, ruggente

con la bocca maledetta d'un soldato,
mentre invocava *Jesu*
e Garibaldi ad un sol fiato.
Ci sono sue reliquie sparse

ovunque nel giardino:
la catena d'oro, i mozziconi spenti,
frantumi di bottiglie,
un badile rotto.

La sua camicia sventola nell'aria.
Lo spaventapasseri indossa la sua fedora.
Sollevo le mie mani a benedir gli uccelli
che su quest'elegie si fiondano veloci.

from fishwives, pulled me from the door.
But after he was drunk,
we all heard him: rasping
his *compline* in dialect, roaring

with the blasted mouth of a soldier,
invoking *Jesu*
and Garibaldi in one breath.
There are relics of him strewn

throughout the garden:
watch chain, cigar stubs,
shards of shattered bottles,
a broken spade.

His shirt flaps in the wind.
The scarecrow wears his fedora.
I lift my hands to bless the birds
that swoop down on these elegies.

Sempre fedele

Riti di stagione

Non è vero
che il peperoncino rosso è il più piccante,
ma quello sottile verde,
il cui fuoco esorcizza la tristezza.
Il mio vegliardo se ne mangia a iosa
con slancio latino.
Lupini in salamoia;
melanzane e mozzarella,
così saporite da infiammare il palato di un felino;
olive nere, finocchio, baccalà;
calamari; alici con la lisca intatta,
litanie e preghiere;
il tutto innaffiato al whiskey.
Ottantasette anni di furia in gola,
rabbia lasciata per la cenere.

+   +   +

Litania

Per un istante è supplicante,
ne è testimone il suo cilicio.
Lui ricorda l'odore dei germogli d'olivo
sparsi per le colline del Foggiano.
Vorrebbe non morire in quest'emisfero,
ma dove la terra riconosce il rantolo del suo perire.
Un uomo che lascia il suo Paese
lo partorisce sempre l'illusione,
senza distinguere mai il singolo attimo dal destino.

Sempre Fidele

Proper of the Season

It is not true
the red pepper is hottest,
but the slender green,
its flame a drug for the spleen.
The old man eats one after another
with Roman élan.
Brine-sopped Lupi beans;
eggplant and Locatelli,
sharp enough to bloody a cat's mouth;
wine olives, fennel, *baccala*;
calamari; smelts,
bone and gristle;
versicle and prayer,
whiskey-coaxed.
Eighty-seven years of fire in his mouth,
anger left for dirt.

+   +   +

Litany

For a moment he is supplicant,
memory his hair shirt.
He recalls the smell of olive blossoms
spreading the hills of Foggia.
He does not wish to die in this hemisphere,
but where the land reckons his death warble.
A man who leaves his country
is forever whelped by illusion,
never knowing whenness from destiny.

Allora attizza il suo vecchio fuoco.
L'imprecazione impera sulla lingua spuria
del whiskey, popola la stanza
come avi in fiamme,
ingurgita vendetta.

+   +   +

Mezzanotte

È il suo buon figlio, mio padre,
che deve metterlo a letto mentre lui infuria
come un Prometeo, privato di fuoco e forgia,
incollerito ad ogni passo dell'aquila.
Le donne lo implorano d'osservar la Pasqua.
Carnevale si avvicina.
Lui fuma a letto, bestemmia.
Il parroco è un *gavone*,
un porco che s'abbuffa.
Una delle sue figlie sta morendo.
In *Italia* sarebbe stato un blasonato;
ed io, luce del suo unico occhio,
mi sentirei d'attraversare gli Appennini
fino al Mediterraneo.

+   +   +

Domenica

All'alba lui zucchera il caffè
con l'anisetta. Poi va in giardino:
dissotterra gli alberi di fico;
pota l'uva canina;
pianta filari di prezzemolo, basilico,
aglio, cipolla, origano.

Then it is the old fire
he threshes. Anathema
prevails upon the spurious tongue
of whiskey, throngs the room
like burning ancestors,
drinks vendetta.

+ + +

Midnight

It is his quiet son, my good father,
who must put him to bed raving
as Prometheus, stripped of fire and forge,
raved at each pass of the eagle.
The women beg him to make Easter Duty.
Shrovetide approaches.
He smokes in bed, blasphemes.
The parish priest is a *gavone,*
un porco who eats too much.
One of his daughters is dying.
In *Italia*, he would have been a baron;
and I, the apple of his only eye,
would cross the Apennines
to the Mediterranean.

+ + +

Sunday

Dawn, he sweetens his coffee
with Anisette. Then to the garden:
exhumes the fig trees;
slashes the fox grape;
plants rows of parsley, *basilico,*
garlic, onion, oregano.

Mi sveglio.
La brina scricchiola sul vetro.
Il mio nome incido nei suoi solchi.
I corvi volano a cerchio sopra il frutteto.
Nuvole scure incombono.
Trovo mio nonno nella sua rimessa,
che fuma il suo Parodi, mentre canta
lo stesso ritornello di una *canzonetta*.
Le campane a messa del mattino fendono le nubi nere.
La terra volge le sue brune tombe al sole,
la donna dimenticata nella collina sbagliata.
Mentre gioco fra le sue scarpe nere,
osservo quel suo occhio orbo,
una visione argentea inglobata,
uno specchio posseduto
dalla sua stessa immagine svanita.

+   +   +

Ninna nanna

Durante la notte, mentre prego che nevichi,
m'assale l'incubo d'essere ubriaco fradicio,
eppure incorruttibile. Ci sono donne
che mi toccano e rispondono alle mie domande.
Mi sveglio che c'è la neve,
di certo la mia novena l'ha evocata.
Per tutto il giorno, fiocchi grandi come ostie
ammorbidiscono gli spigoli del mondo.
Non ho voglia di giocare, voglio rimanere solo.
Mentre scavo un solco nella membrana nevosa,
trovo un pertugio.
Mi si rapprende il sangue. Una complicità strana
con quest'elemento mi ingiunge di dormire.
Mi chiamano; ma sono trasportato via,
fuori dalla loro presa, sovrano.

I wake.
Hoarfrost cracks on my window.
I scrape into its welts my name.
Crows circle the orchard.
Thunderheads well.
I find my grandfather in his shed,
smoking Parodis, singing
the same two lines of a *canzonetta*.
Early mass bells split the black clouds.
Earth turns its brown graves to the sun,
the forgotten woman in the wrong hill.
Playing between his black shoes,
I watch that bad eye of his,
some vision silvered beneath,
a mirror possessed
by its own whelmed image.

+   +   +

Lullaby

Through the night, praying for snow,
I have nightmares in which I'm dead drunk,
but incorruptible. Women
touch me and answer my questions.
I wake to snow,
sure my novena conjured it.
All day, flakes big as half-dollars
softening the world's angles.
I don't want to play, but be alone.
As I burrow into the white meninx,
there is a crossing over.
My blood knots. A strange fealty
for this element adjures me to sleep.
They call; but I am drifted over,
outside them, sovereign.

+   +   +

Memento Mori

Seduto tra mio padre e mia sorella,
premo le ginocchia sul pannello caldo nella Plymouth del '56.
Il vivaio dei Gumto ha un bel calore,
ma l'odore mesto dei fiori mi dà il voltastomaco.
Marie conosce il nome di ogni specie floreale.
Per noi, è un gioco:
la nostra visita quaresimale al camposanto di S. Pietro,
mentre aiutiamo nostro padre a rintracciare
l'atavico pezzo di terra di sua madre;
la sua porzione d'America, qui in questo cimitero
per errore, unica tra le tombe luterane;
soffocata dal rampicante e le campanule.
Nel salire dietro a lui arranchiamo.
Ficco il mio piede nelle sue impronte.
Ogni anno il loculo esatto ci elude,
il mucchietto d'ossa che immagino mi voglia bene.
La vecchia croce traballante, il nome
Battiante—mezzo cancellato.
Mio padre sega i rametti di pino,
inserisce i chiodi che io possa battere.
Marie scrive sulla nuova croce il nome
della sua omonima: *Maria Cristina*.

Le piantine inzollate e annaffiate,
mio padre non ci chiede di pregare.
Accucciato vicino alla tomba
sulla fiancata ripida, ci abbraccia.
Abbiamo ereditato questo lotto,
il peccato veniale di suo padre,
che sbircia maligno dalla sua cornea opaca.
Vediamo il fiume Allegheny

+   +   +

Memento Mori

I sit between my father and sister,
knees pressed to our '56 Plymouth's heater.
Gumto's Greenhouse is warm,
but its sad smell of flowers turns my stomach.
Marie can name each genus.
To us, it is a game:
our Lenten office at Saint Peter's,
helping our father find
his mother's moiety of feudal dirt;
her cantle of America, here in this cemetery
by mistake, alone among Lutherans;
choked by catbrier and morning glory.
We trudge uphill behind him.
I fit my boot into each print he makes.
Each year the plot eludes us,
the trove of bones I imagine loves me.
The old cross keens, half the name—
Battiante—obscured.
My father saws the pine strips,
taps in the nails for me to pound. Marie
letters upon the new cross the name
of her namesake: *Maria Cristina.*

Seedlings rooted and watered,
my father does not make us pray.
From a squat at the steep
grave-head, he holds us.
We've inherited this land,
his father's venial blunder, leering
blasted from the opaque cornea.
We watch the Allegheny

spingersi a ovest verso l'equinozio,
i suoi declivi circostanti sfigurati dalla neve.
Scendendo giù dalla collina, troviamo
un fagiano morto e seppelliamo pure quello.
Se fossi lasciato qui, non troverei mai la via di casa,
vagherei, bambino per sempre,
in questa strana cava di fantasmi a me sconosciuti.
Placo la pietra in un tripudio
di *Ave Maria e Gloria*—
già dispiaciuto per ogni fatto accaduto.

+   +   +

Festa dell'Assunzione, 1920

I Papisti nelle strade appostati per le loro stregonerie.
Gli accoliti trasportano lo stendardo blu di Nostra Signora
trapunto di dollari,
gli incensieri spargono mirra e incenso.
La banda suona.
Gli immigrati cantano dai gradini di casa:
Ave Maria, Regina Coeli.
Sopra, in una stanzetta, una donna è morta di parto.
Un bambino ancora troppo giovane per la penitenza
guarda sua madre sollevata
dalla planca mortuaria e il suo corpo portato
a braccio nelle strade in festa.
Anche la terra rabbrividisce.
Sua madre levita
sopra i portatori dai guanti grigi.

+   +   +

pushing west toward the equinox,
its surrounding slopes mauled by snow.
Back down the hill, we find
a dead pheasant and bury it too.
Left here, I would never find my way home,
wandering, forever a child,
in this odd quarry of unfamiliar ghosts.
I placate stone in a blaze
of *Hail Marys* and *Glory Bes*—
already sorry for everything.

+   +   +

The Feast of The Assumption, 1920

The Papists are at their sorcery in the streets.
Acolytes carry Our Lady's blue banner
tacked with dollar bills,
censers seething myrrh and frankincense.
The band plays.
Immigrants sing from the stoops:
Ave Maria, Regina Coeli.
Above them, in a small room,
a woman is dead to childbirth.
A boy too young to confess
watches his mother lifted
from the cooling board and carried
into the dancing streets.
The earth too shudders.
His mother levitates
above the gray-gloved bearers.

+   +   +

Nunc Dimittis

Correndo via dall'orto di mio nonno,
inciampo in un groviglio della vigna
e dalla soglia del mio mondo sprofondo
nel giardino dei ciliegi. Canticchiando *O Bambino*,
il nonno mi trova, grida, *Gesù Cristo*;
poi, a passi sghembi, invoca l'aiuto
di mio padre con quel po' d'inglese che conosce,
e lui arriva di gran corsa.
L'anziano aspetta che lui mi sollevi.
Per un istante, pregano per me,
poi insieme delicatamente
tolgono dal mio viso i resti
del frutto spiaccicato. Il mio sangue
tonfa a terra, un obolo
che la terra accetta
al di là della provenienza e genealogia—
la nostra genìa foglia di sangue.

Nunc Dimittis

Running from my grandfather's garden,
I catch in a skein of grape vine
and crash through the lintel of my world
into the cherry orchard. Humming *O Bambino*,
he comes upon me, shrieks,
Gesu Cristo; then crabs off, hailing
in his matrix of English my father
who comes galloping.
The old man waits for him to lift me.
For a moment, they pray
over me, then together
gently pick the pits and spalls
of fruit from my face. My blood
thuds to earth, a pittance
of shrift the earth accepts
beyond provenance and ancestry—
our blood-leaf.

Larimer Avenue

È lunga un miglio, dodici isolati—dritto per Highland,
poi a sinistra a Saint Marie

dove le case stanno accucciate in fila
e muratori e stuccatori, grigi di cemento,

si trascinano a casa per la cena.
I ragazzini giocano a baseball nel cortile della scuola.

Le prime bottiglie fanno la comparsa da Chookie's Corner.
I vecchi pensosi si dondolano nella loggetta.

Loro lo sanno dove stiamo andando:
passando per Meadow Street Bridge fin dentro le viscere della progenie—

Larimer Avenue, dove ogni John si crede un gangster.
Corrotti politicanti—che intimidiscono con i cappelli Stetson,

e i completi eleganti—dinoccolati stanno sulla porta di Genevieve.
Seguendo i loro passi, apprendisti bambini,

schivano macchine, lanciano monetine, giocano ai dadi al riparo
    delle mura dei bar.
I negozianti bruschi chiudono bottega, si insultano a vicenda

in calabrese e piemontese.
Il vecchio Labriola avanza cauto sul marciapiede,

si guarda alle spalle temendo un'imboscata,
copre i barili di olive, sospettoso

ripone forme di provolone e salame
nel suo negozio che sa di chiuso. Mercoledì delle ceneri:

Larimer Avenue

It's a mile drive, twelve city blocks—down
Highland, then left at Saint Marie

where houses squat in rows and bricklayers
and cement finishers, grayed

with mortar, slump home to supper.
Kids play Indian-ball in the schoolyard.

The first bottles unsheath on Chookie's corner.
Old men think on porch gliders.

They know where we're going:
across Meadow Street Bridge into the gut of ancestry—

Larimer Avenue, where every John thinks he's a gangster.
Tinhorn politicians—snap-brim Stetsons, menacing

suits—slouch in Genevieve's doorway.
In their shadow, children apprentice,

dodging cars, pitching pennies and craps in corner joint lees.
Crusty merchants close shop, harangue one another

in *Calabrese* and *Piedmontese*.
Old man Labriola sidles warily onto the sidewalk,

checks his flanks as if expecting ambush,
covers the olive barrels, suspiciously

lugs hanging tuns of provolone and salami
back into his musty store. Ash Wednesday:

Alfred DiStefano, mentre gustava le sue ultime olive siciliane
dal barile di Labby, beccò sei pallottole

in pancia da una Caddy fantasma—proprio lì
sul cemento in un miscuglio di sangue e olio d'oliva.

Noi stiamo seduti nei soliti quattro posti della Belair Chevrolet del '63.
Facce tristi di neri e latini guardano dalle finestre:

nelle soffitte sovrastanti Paradise e Costa;
a Stoebner Alley, tappezzato di bottiglie vuote—

Manischevitts, Wild Irish Rose. Più avanti
attraverso Larimer Bridge—l'aria addolcita dal forno Rimini—

in quello stesso ponte Charles Harris,
inseguito dai pastori tedeschi di Chester

dopo aver derubato la pompa di benzina, fuggendo
s'era buttato giù—rompendosi solo una gamba.

Alfred DiStefano, eating his last Sicilian olives
from Labby's barrels, took six neat ones

in the belly from a phantom Caddy—right there
on the cement in a suite of blood and olive oil.

The four of us sit in familiar quadrants of our '63 Belair.
Long black and Latin faces stare from each window:

in the garrets above Paradise and Costa;
in Stoebner Alley, trashed with old soldiers—

Manischewitz, Wild Irish Rose. On across
Larimer Bridge—Rimini's Bakery sweetening the air—

over which Charles Harris,
chased by Chester's German Shepherds

after he robbed the station, hurled himself
to escape—and only broke a leg.

La lapide

Mio padre non ha mai parlato tanto.
Suo padre, morto oggi, dopo novantuno anni,
faceva lo stesso. Ranicchiato sulla poltrona del barbiere,
non ricordo una sola parola tra di loro.

Fred mi alza e mi gira, intimandomi
di star fermo o farà del mio orecchio un posacenere.
Racconta barzellette oscene e mi stuzzica sulle ragazze.
Le chiama *femmine*.

Dallo specchio strizza l'occhio a mio padre,
che staziona sul piedistallo dello sciuscià,
distratto in apparenza.
"Non aveva forse una bottega il tuo vecchio,

lì a Mayflower?" chiede Fred.
Mio padre non risponde *sì*, né dice *no*.
"Era una gran simpaticone, vero?"
Mi chiedo perché mio padre non zittisca questo barbiere.

Eppure sento il peso incombente del silenzio.
Mio nonno ha sempre rifiutato di parlare inglese.
Quando sollevava la mano gli altri capivano
che aveva finito. Beveva un altro sorso

e non guardava più nessuno.
Non so qual era la faccenda
tra lui e mio padre.
Fred con il suo rasoio solca il mio sguardo sullo specchio,

in riflesso gli operai che finito il turno alla Peabody
si avvicinano alla pizza "da Vento."
Mio padre prende il mio posto sulla poltrona
mentre io mi rifugio nel retrobottega

The Headstone

My father has never talked much.
His father, dead today, after ninety-one years,
was the same. Tucked in the barber's chair,
I can't remember a single sentence passed between them.

Fred jacks me up and spins me, grumbling
to keep still or I'll be using my ear for an ashtray.
He tells dirty jokes and kids me about girls.
He calls them *broads*.

Through the mirror he winks at my father,
lounging on the shoeshine stand,
not appearing to pay attention.
"Didn't your old man run a shop

down on Mayflower?" Fred asks.
My father does not say *yes*, does not say *no*.
"He was a real sport. Wasn't he?"
I wonder why he doesn't correct this barber.

Yet I feel the pall of silence stealing over me.
My grandfather refused to speak English.
We knew when he lifted his hand,
he was finished. He drank wine

and no longer looked at anyone.
I don't know what went on
between him and my father.
Fred's razor rivets my mirrored stare,

reflecting a dismissed Peabody shift
strolling toward Vento's Pizza.
My father replaces me in the chair
as I wander into the back

dove Frankie, lo sciuscià, sta accomodato
su una pila di *Playboys* a scrivere numeri.
Sono tentato di scommettere un dollaro
sulla data di nascita di mio nonno.

Tutti quegli anni, avvolto nel telo
in quella poltrona cromata porcellanata,
ho sentito chi scommetteva giurare
sulle loro madri rese sante

che un numero giocato su un morto di sicuro vince.
Mio padre sta seduto su quella poltrona,
accanto alla finestra, la luce del sole inonda
il telo bianco sulle spalle,

controluce risaltano le sue ciocche nere.
Non ho voluto chiedergli se il Nonno morendo avesse avuto un prete.
Di ritorno a casa, ci fermiamo per un hotdog da "L'Originale."
Moe, il proprietario, dice a mio padre:

"Mi dispiace per il tuo vecchio,"
poi gli fa un cenno, "Questo è tuo figlio?"
L'ultima tappa è per cercare la pietra tombale.
Pofi sta seduto nel suo piazzale tra le lapidi,

il sole brilla sull'aggregato argenteo.
Fa lo stesso mestiere di suo padre.
Ancora usa gli attrezzi portati dal vecchio con sé da Napoli.
S'alza per stringere la mano di mio padre.

"Una brutta faccenda," dice. "Che ci vuoi scrivere sopra?"
Siccome la risposta di mio padre non arriva,
si gira verso di me e mi chiede
"Che ci vuoi scritto sopra?"

where Frankie, the Shine, plops
on a stack of *Playboys*, writing numbers.
I'm tempted to lay a buck
on my grandfather's birth date.

All those years, shrouded
in that big chrome and porcelain chair,
I've listened to bookies swear
on their sainted mothers

that a number played on a corpse is sure to hit.
My father sits in the chair
in the window, sunlight streaming
down the slopes of the white sheet,

his clipped hair black against it.
I haven't wanted to ask him if Papa had a priest.
On the way home, we stop for hotdogs at The Original.
Moe, the owner, says to my dad:

"Sorry about your old man,"
then nods, "Is that your kid?"
Our last stop is to see about the stone.
Pofi sits in his yard among the markers,

sun glittering in the silver aggregate.
It was his father's business.
He still uses the tools the old man brought over from Naples.
He gets up to shake hands with my father.

"This is a hell of a thing," he says. "What do you want on it?"
When after a while my father doesn't answer,
he looks at me and asks,
"What do you want on it?"

Miglior vita

—Paolo Battiante
(1877–1968)

A mille chilometri dalla Puglia,
il mare è un oracolo
che s'attorciglia sulla trinca della nave:

avrò un figlio che non amerà l'acqua.
Il suo nome sarà sottratto.
Non importa.

Rimarrò sconosciuto.
Dove vivo, uno straniero
anche per i fantasmi che mi trafiggono,

è buio senza la vista
dell'occhio estirpato dall'arcione
nell'ultima incursione garibaldina.

Il suo ultimo barlume—
il mio stallone in fiamme, uno spaventapasseri
avvolto nella camicia rubiconda del Condottiero,

rossa la mela che teneva Maria—
ora l'occhio percosso
nei marosi del golfo di Taranto.

Non presumere il mio dolore, né la mia lingua.
Ciò che rimane dell'amore mette radici.
Un seme gettato col mio sputo prospera.

Salpo per l'America con cazzuola
e martello, un occhio solo, nessuna voce.
Ai miei figlioli lascio in eredità il silenzio—

A Better Life

—Paolo Battiante
(1877–1968)

A thousand kilometers from Apulia,
the sea is an oracle
coiling at the gunwales:

I will have a son who will not love water.
His name will be taken.
No matter.

I will remain unknown.
Where I live unacquainted
even with the ghosts who needle me,

it is dark without the sight
of the eye plucked by pig-iron
on my last ride with Garibaldi.

Its final glimpse—
my stallion afire, a scarecrow
wrapped in the Padrone's red blouse,

Maria holding a red apple—
yet swills in a trench
along the Gulf of Taranto.

Do not suppose my grief, nor language.
What love remains is planted.
A seed dropped in my spit prospers.

I sail to America with trowel
and hammer, one eye, no voice.
To my children I bequeath silence—

ciò che di me detesteranno,
e che da soli dovranno fendere,
il cuneo di questo mare di pietra che hanno dentro.

Dio non mi ha preparato per questo paese maledetto.
La mia mano lo rigetta.
Ci faccia pace la mia progenie.

what they will loathe in me,
and have to break alone like the wedge
of this stone sea in themselves.

God did not prepare me for this bitch country.
My hand is against it.
Let my blood make peace.

Graziella

Il suo scrutinio silenzioso e serio
della verdura a mercato nero

mi faceva temere che
potessi attirare il suo malocchio

e finire arrostito come i suoi peperoni.
Quando lei spuntava, con i capelli raccolti a crocchia

come un carapace nero, divinatorio,
che intimava pentimento,

i nostri giochi si interrompevano al suo lutto:
robuste scarpe nere in marcia

giorno dopo giorno al passo
con le campane della chiesa, barattando

i sacramenti per l'anima del suo compianto
Napoletano; a Monte Carmelo, raspando

nella terra del sepolcro, mormorava
antifone sotto un cielo azzurro,

ingobbita sulla tomba, le dita
attorcinate nei rosari, a sbriciolare

ogni zolla indifferente, cercando
il polso forte del suo amante, rovesciando

i gerani, dando la parola
ad ogni pietra, lei mi impala

sulla croce
della mia mortalità.

Graziella

Her grave silent scrutiny
of the huckster's vegetables

made me wary,
lest I speck her evil eye

and be roasted like peppers.
When she appeared, hair netted

like a black carapace, soothsaying,
penance-hawking,

our games fell to her mourning:
hard black shoes soldiering

one after another each day
to church bells, bartering

with the sacraments for the soul of her lost
Napolitano; at Mount Carmel, scrabbling

through grave dirt, mumbling
antiphonies beneath a blue sky,

hunched over the tomb, hands
strapped with rosaries, crumbling

each indifferent clod, searching
for her lover's fist, upsetting

the geraniums, giving utterance
to each stone, impaling

me on the spine
of my own mortality.

Lincoln Avenue

Dalla nostra palazzina bifamiliare,
intersecata da camere mortuarie e templi africani,
osservavo spettacolari veglie.

Proibito attraversar la strada, proibito
girare l'angolo, mappavo
la mia porzione di cemento, studiando

muri cosparsi di *fanculo e sporco negro*,
contro i quali infermiere e marmisti
languivano in attesa

dell'ultimo tram su per Cemetery Hill.
Avevo smesso di credere alla fata madrina
e polverizzavo i denti da latte sulle rotaie del tram.

Ruote d'acciaio su binari d'acciaio
incastonati tra sanpietrini da cinque chili stridevano
e facevano scintille mentre i tramvai

trasportavano passeggeri appesi alle maniglie
diretti alle locande e ai bar sulla collina
dove Joe Westray costruì The Ebony Lounge

a fianco della chiesa del Corpus Christi.
Sorseggiando bottigliette di birra Iron City,
i tipi allisciati stavano seduti

sul marciapiede su sedie ripieghevoli
occhieggiando la nostra auto scassata
mentre ci portava arrancando verso casa.

Lincoln Avenue

From our Lincoln duplex, crosscut
by black mortuaries and African temples,
I watched spectacular wakes.

Forbidden across the street, forbidden
around the corner, I mapped
my allotment of concrete, studying

walls sprayed with *fuck* and *nigger*,
against which nurses and stonecutters
died as they waited

for the last trolley up Cemetery Hill.
I had given up on my fairy godmother
and powdered my milk-teeth on the tracks.

Steel wheels on steel rails rutted
in gray ten-pound cobbles screeched
and sparked as streetcars

freighted straphangers to rib joints
and storefront clubs on the Hill
where Joe Westray built The Ebony Lounge

next to The Church of Corpus Christi.
Sipping Iron City ponies,
guys with processes sat

on curbs in folding chairs
eyeing our heap
as it lumbered us home.

Messo a letto mentre era ancora giorno, pregavo
di addormentarmi prima di avere incubi,
certo di sentire spari di sopra

dall'ex-poliziotto dopo la sbornia di whiskey
venduto sottobanco, sua sorella che gridava
"quei delinquenti neri" gli avevano avvelenato l'alcol.

La notte che il suo cuore esplose,
un celerino lo raccolse, mentre inondava di rosso sangue
la mia stanza con la sirena.

Bedded while still light, I prayed
to sleep before nightmare,
certain I heard gunfire upstairs

from the ex-cop sleeping off speakeasy
whiskey, his sister screaming
"those black thugs" had poisoned his booze.

The night his heart exploded,
a paddy wagon fetched him, splashing
my room with its bloody siren.

Prometeo

Quando finalmente tolgono l'ingessatura,
invece del braccio di mio padre, ce n'è uno sconosciuto:
color indaco brunito, inciso
dal polso al gomito, glabro,

con una lunga rabberciata scritta creata
dal filo chirurgico che non riesco a decifrare.
Con il suo braccio buono, sistema l'altro,
un peso morto, come un bambino sprofondato nel sonno

che lo si vuole portare a letto senza svegliarlo.
Persino dopo che sono tolti i punti,
il braccio rimane fermo là, denunciando mio padre
la sua incisione, trattata con burro di cacao,

che minaccia di aprirsi e sputar fuori
i suoi filamenti rossi aggrovigliati,
tagliati maledettamente da un ellissoide
di metallo schizzato in aria.

La sua mano vuota e gelida, resta insensibile.
Per misurare la sua forza, stringe la mia mano,
ma senza la sua solita energia,
e sorridendo la fa cadere.

Nella sua vestaglia, le notti, da solo, a fumare,
sorseggiando vino rosso, cercando di decantare
i frantumati calici del sangue perduto,
il libro che non gli interessa riposto sul comodino,

Prometheus

When finally the cast comes off,
in place of my father's arm is a stranger's:
blackened indigo, inscribed
wrist to elbow, hairless,

with a long, hyphenated catgut sentence
I'm unable to read. With his good arm,
he arranges it, its peculiar density,
like a deeply sleeping baby

one tries to bed without waking.
Even after the stitches come out,
the arm just lies there, denouncing
my father, its cocoa-buttered

incision threatening to open any moment
and push out its mangled red wires,
accidentally stripped by an ellipsoid
of jack-knifed aluminum.

Its empty icy hand has no feeling.
To test its strength, he squeezes
my hand, then simply smiles
without his might and drops it.

In his robe, nights, alone, smoking,
sipping red wine, trying to decant
the smashed goblets of blood lost,
the book he has no interest in laid aside,

con una voce a me ignota,
parla alla sua mano,
la apre e chiude su una palla di gomma,
l'avvicina alla sigaretta accesa.

Cerchi di fumo salgono fino al pianerottolo dove mi nascondo.
Al suo primo turno di rientro all'altoforno, la mano rinnegata,
sfiora una fornace a carbone e il guanto prende fuoco.
Ma non sente nulla.

Nella sua tuta di amianto, continua a mescolare
la massa infuocata fino a che un altro mastro operaio
lo vede e grida. Mio padre solleva la visiera
e fissa le sue dita che sputano fuoco—

così in un modo surreale sorride ai compagni
che con le mani cercano di spegnergli le fiamme,
e innalza verso il cielo della notte d'acciaio
la sua mano infuocata.

he talks to the hand, opening
and closing around a rubber ball,
in a voice I've never heard.
He holds his cigarette to it.

Smoke rises to my hiding place on the landing.
His first swing back at the Basic Oxygen Plant,
the reneged hand, gloved, brushes a coke forge
and ignites. He feels nothing.

In his asbestos tunic, he goes on ladling
heat until another millwright cries out.
My father lifts his mask and stares
at his fingers guttering fire—

so favoring dream he smiles upon
the slag-gang slapping at him
and hoists into the steel night sky
his flaming hand.

Figlio di un prete

L'anno che ero in terza elementare,
mio padre, inframezzando
gli scioperi di fabbrica con lavoretti saltuari,

faceva il custode nella parrocchia di San Pietro e Paolo.
Nessuna suora osava picchiarmi
con lui che si aggirava nei paraggi.

Loro lo amavano proprio come si fa coi preti—
un uomo in pieno controllo di tutta la struttura,
che possedeva le chiavi d'ogni porta sacramentale.

Guidava lo spazzaneve e beveva con il Pastore.
Il giorno prima delle Ceneri,
ammantava tutti i Santi

con i drappi viola della Quaresima;
poi li riponeva via quaranta giorni dopo
nelle ore piccole

prima che Cristo ritornasse.
Ripuliva tutti i luoghi ascosi; ed io,
da vero figlio di un prete, lo seguivo

nel controllo della fortezza sacra.
Mettevo la mia faccia davanti al tabernacolo,
mi infilavo dietro l'altare dorato

(disperato che fosse di legno),
rovistavo negli armadi della sacrestia:
calice, paramenti, turiboli, ampolline.

Son of a Priest

The year I was in third grade,
my father, who bided steel
strikes by odd-jobbing,

janitored at Saints Peter and Paul.
No nun dared strike me
with him in the building.

They loved him the way they loved
priests—a man with the run of things,
keys to every sacramental door.

He drove the snowplow and drank
with the Pastor. On Shrove
Tuesday, he placed over the Communion

of Saints the purple rags
of abnegation; then snatched them
off forty days later in the little hours

of Christ's comeback. He cleansed
the secret places; and I,
like the son of a priest, followed him

to reckon the holy fortress.
I put my face to the tabernacle,
squeezed behind the golden altar

(distraught it was made of wood),
rummaged the sacristy cabinets:
chalice, vestments, thurible, cruets.

Presso l'altare di Nostra Signora, accendendo
tutte le candele votive, le baciavo i piedi.
Ogni oggetto sacro, lo toccavo.

Lavavo la mia faccia nell'acqua benedetta,
la bevevo a sorsi. Salivo sul pulpito.
Avvolto nella stola del Confessore,

mi accomodavo sulla sua sedia del perdono—
dove una volta mi spaventai, e andai a cercare mio padre,
che passava la spugna nel santuario

o stava arrampicato su una scala,
a spolverare il Crocefisso Gigante.
Rassicurato, sgattaiolavo nella Cappella di S. Giuseppe,

dove mi avevano battezzato,
e mi addormentavo
sull'unico panchetto dal cuscinetto rosso.

At Our Lady's altar, I lit each votive
and kissed her feet.
Every sacred object, I touched.

I washed my face in holy water,
sipped it. I mounted the pulpit.
Wrapped in the Confessor's stole,

I lounged in his forgiving chair—
where I got scared, and went looking
for my father, swabbing the sanctuary

or high on a ladder, dusting
the mammoth Crucifix. Relieved,
I slunk into Saint Joseph's Chapel,

where I was baptized,
and fell asleep
on its single red-cushioned pew.

Cresima

Suor Simon ci aveva torturato
per settimane intere con le domande
che il Vescovo poteva chiederci a casaccio.

Avevo imparato a memoria le parti principali della Messa,
i sacri calici, i liturgici colori,
le ricorrenze,

tutte le basiliche di Roma. Ma il Vescovo
non ci chiese nulla; si limitò a un colpetto distratto
e ci impresse il segno del crisma con mano tremante.

Ricordo solo che si chiamava Thomas,
che la sua mitra verde traballava
mentre mi chiedeva che nome avessi scelto.

Il mio padrino indossava una cravatta bianca
e afferrò forte la mia spalla. D'un tratto
ero diventato un soldato nell'Esercito di Cristo,

ma non smettevo di pensare alle ragazze della mia classe;
i loro lunghi capelli lisci e i corpi consacrati.
Avevo scelto il nome di un uomo

che era diventato Re di Francia a quindici anni
e condotto due crociate in Terra Santa.
Che ne sapevo

di come gli uomini si gettavano nella pugna e nell'amore?Durante il
ricevimento, mi diedero dei soldi.
Le zie mi baciarono. Gli zii mi strinsero la mano

Confirmation

Sister Simon grilled us
for weeks on the questions
the Bishop might ask at random.

I memorized the principle parts of the Mass,
the sacred vessels, Liturgical
colors, commemorations,

the stational churches of Rome.
But the Bishop asked nothing;
gave but a dry slap and palsied stamp of chrism.

I remember only that his name was Thomas,
that his green miter shook
as he asked what name I had chosen.

My Godfather wore a white tie
and clamped my shoulder. Suddenly
a soldier in The Army of Christ,

I couldn't stop thinking of the girls in my class:
their long straight hair and consecrated bodies.
I had taken the name of a man

who became King of France at age fifteen
and led two crusades to the Holy Land.
What did I know

of how men fought and loved?
At the party, I was given money.
Aunts kissed me. Uncles shook my hand

inducendomi poi a un sorso di whiskey.
Tutto quello che desideravo era restare solo.
Nei filmetti di famiglia, appaio come un ragazzo dolce

che indossa una giacca rossa, con in mano
una bottiglia di Lord Calvert,
e tutti intorno a me che ridono.

and coaxed me into a shot of whiskey.
All I wanted was to be alone.
In the home movies, I'm a sweet boy

in red blazer, holding a bottle
of Lord Calvert,
everyone about me laughing.

Kyrie

Seguo le regole in silenzio,
il corpo posseduto dall'anima di un discolo,
sperando che la pietà posticcia

della moglie di Cristo non si materializzi
in una bacchettata sulla mia guancia
mentre fingo di non sapere ciò che so benissimo,

poiché ho segretamente letto i libri di mia sorella,
e ho più parole che mi frullano in testa
di questi esperti millantatori

che tracciano pagine su pagine
di Gesuiti all'Offertorio
in vestimenti porpora.

Ho fatto un patto col diavolo, lei mi dice,
i suoi occhi neri come la pece, bellissima:
con soggolo e scarpe pesanti,

calze nere, un imponente rosario.
Le lavagne sono piene di mie punizioni—
Sono un ragazzaccio maledetto peccatore—

polvere di gesso che mi soffoca,
i miei pugni totalmente bianchi.
La sua astuzia mi toglie il fiato,

ma davvero non so trattenere il sorriso
che mi sale furtivo sulle labbra dal profondo
mentre prego per la salvezza,

Kyrie

Dumbly I toe my mark,
body possessed of a bad boy's soul,
hoping the strained mercy

of Christ's wife will not crack
like a stick cross my cheek
as I pretend not to know what I know best,

having secretly read my sister's books
and have more words haunting my head
than these expert tattlers

drawing page upon perfect page
of Jesuits at Offertory
in purple vestments.

I've had truck with the devil,
she says, raven-eyed, gorgeous:
wimple and jackboot oxfords,

black hose, big rosary.
The blackboards circle with my penitent script—
I am cursed a sinful boy—

chalk dust gagging me,
my fists white.
Her stealth takes my breath,

but truly I cannot check the smile
that steals to my lips on the lane from my soul
as I pray for deliverance, cocking

prestando orecchio agli ubriachi a Flavel Street,
che mi tirano le bottiglie vuote
contro alle inferriate nere.

an ear to the drunks on Flavel Street,
hailing me with empty pints
against the black iron grate.

Lo Sprofondo

I nostri vecchi italiani lo chiamavano con una parola,
che suonava come "Lo Sprofondo," ma con più *fondo*,
più *dolore* in esso—
quasi *sacrale*:

Bassa La Vallone.
Io non riuscivo a pronunciarlo,
ma è lì che andavo quando volevo
stare solo, incurante del pericolo di

serpenti e Spacaluccio—il mostro che viveva
ai piedi di Meadow Street Bridge,
sopra Lo Sprofondo, e
che divorava i bimbi ribelli.

Il mio bosco, un corridoio di arbusti e meli selvatici
attaccato a Negley Run, s'incuneava
tra i dirupi di desideri mescolati:
di neri ed immigrati.

Combattevano con sassi e rametti,
gridandosi da una parte all'altra dell'abisso,
sopra la cima degli alberi, sotto cui mi ranicchiavo,
mentre scolpivo arco e frecce col mio primo coltello

dal sottile tronco di sommacco con i suoi rami.
Nello Sprofondo i ragazzacci costruivano case
sugli alberi per portarci le ragazze—
quelle bionde con le ciglia nere

(*quelle toste*, mia madre le chiamava),
mio Dio, loro mi facevano tremare:
ragazze che incidevano con pezzi di bottiglia
tatuaggi casarecci sui bicipiti dei fidanzati—

The Hollow

The old Italian people had a word
for it that sounded like *hollow*,
but with more *hole*, more *woe*
in it—like *holy*:

Bassa La Vallone.
I could not pronounce it,
but it's where I went when I wanted
to be alone despite warnings

of snakes and Spacaluccio—
the monster that lived beneath Meadow Street
Bridge, spanning the Hollow—
and fed on disobedient children.

My woods, a swath of sumac
and crabapples stuck to the shoulder
of Negley Run, was wedged between
cliffs of mixed hungers: black and immigrant.

They fought with rocks and sticks, and screamed
across the abyss at each other, over tops
of trees, under which I huddled, skinning
a bow and arrows with my first knife

the slender sumac trunk and branches.
In the Hollow the hoods built tree houses
to take their girls—
those black-lashed blondes (*hard*,

my mother called them), Jesus,
that made the green about me flutter:
girls who scabbed with broken bottles
homemade tattoos into their boyfriends' biceps—

una croce con fiammelle ai lati;
poi le iniziali, *L. A.*, che stavano per Larimer Avenue—
e friggevano gli scoiattoli uccisi con i piombini.
Che ci facevo là—trascinato senza tregua

sempre più giù nello splendente verde,
mentre bevevo acqua dalla pietra,
senza ripararmi dalla pioggia né emetter suono,
mangiando solo quelle melette

che sapevano tanto di lingua straniera?
Quando emergevo dai cespugli,
i padri stavano appena ritornando a casa
dal lavoro; il traffico aumentava.

Camminando per il vialone,
sentivo sbattere le portiere delle macchine
lungo Collins Avenue,
poi sentivo il mio nome chiamato

da mia madre, sulla veranda
con mio padre. Esitavo un poco
prima di rendermi visibile.
Le cose sarebbero presto cambiate,

lo sapevo. Ma niente
era ancora cambiato fino
a quel momento,
quell'ultimo istante in cui non sapevo

chi fossi o chi sarei stato—
sapendo solo che c'erano due mondi:
quello con *me* e quello con *loro*,
e che io stavo in quello mio.

a cross with a tongue of flame in each right angle;
then initials, *L.A.*, for Larimer Avenue—
and fried the squirrels they killed with BBs.
What was I doing there—drawn incessantly

deeper into the white gleaming green,
drinking water from a stone,
not getting in from the rain nor making a sound,
eating only the tiny apples

that tasted so much of a foreign tongue?
When I emerged from the thicket,
fathers were just arriving home from work;
traffic picked up.

Walking along the Run,
I heard car doors slamming
up and down Collins Avenue,
then my name coming at me

from my mother, on the porch
with my father. I hesitated
before allowing myself to be seen.
Things would soon change,

I knew. But nothing
had then yet changed,
not at that minute,
that last minute when I didn't know

who I was or what I'd be—
only that there were two worlds:
one of *I,* one of *they,*
and that I was the one.

La strega

Dopo la mascalzonata, lei restava in piedi
sui vetri rotti nel suo cortile pieno di fuliggine

a Shakespeare Street—
lì tiravamo pietre per rompere

le finestre di fonderie dismesse,
l'odore dolciastro della National Biscuit

glassava ogni pila di mattoni e metallo torto.
Il nostro gioco favorito era uccidere.

I nostri libri preferiti, la morte.
C'era stato inculcato:

Dio è Amore.
E non la sua faccia rugosa e

le mantelle attorcigliate, che s'innervavano
nel nudo cielo, per toccarci,

ma non la vedevamo
perché nei nostri occhi c'era sangue.

Né sentivamo la monodia
provenire dalle impoverite labbra

della follia, per quella fuga d'amore
di tanto tempo fa prima di noi—

The Witch

She stood for what we did
on broken glass in her soot yard

on Shakespeare Street—
ours to stone on the way to break

windows in vacant foundries,
the pall of sweets from National Biscuit

glazing each pile of bricks and twisted metal.
Our favorite games were killing.

Our favorite books were death.
It had been beaten into us:

God is Love.
Not the parched face and gnarled

capes, jittering in the nude
sky, we could not see trying

to touch us for the blood in our eyes.
Nor could we hear the monody

from the impoverished lips of madness
eloped with before our births—

sentivamo solo i suoi incantesimi sdentati
basta, per piacere,

zittiti dal rimbalzo delle castagne
tirate alla sua unica stanza stregata.

only her toothless incantations
of *stop* and *please*, muted

by the buckeyes rifling
off her one-room haunted house.

La morte di East Liberty

Il Cattolico era stato assassinato,
la sua Frontiera spazzata via

da vetri e mattoni ridotti in polvere.
La sfera distruttrice svuotò il cielo come una bomba atomica.

Metà degli elettori non parlava inglese
per poter salvare le loro case. Sputavano

sul marciapiede e maledicevano i politicanti
per i quali s'erano accodati ai seggi,

per assicurare un lavoro ai figli.
Le donne, anche loro a pezzi, accesero candele

torcendosi le mani. Gli uomini sedevano
sulle macerie piangendo con i martelli pneumatici.

Gli alberi furono sradicati e le case
stese giù come ubriachi derubati.

Alla fine se ne andarono, presero i cinquemila
come baratto delle loro vite,

e fecero buon viso per un nuovo inizio.
Ma la demolizione s'era insinuata nelle vene,

affidandosi a silenzio e distruzione per punire amore.
La memoria rarefazione della vendetta.

Gli italiani andavano muti nelle loro tombe,
completamente atterriti dall'America.

The Death of East Liberty

The Catholic had been assassinated,
his Frontier swept away

by glass and brick dust.
The wrecking ball emptied the sky like an atom bomb.

Half the voters could not speak English
to save their homes. They spit

on the sidewalk and cursed the tinhorn
politicos they'd queued at the polls for

to keep their kids employed.
Women lit candles and went to pieces

with their hands. The men sat in rubble
and wept with the jackhammers.

Trees were plucked and houses
bowled over like fleeced drunks.

In the end they moved, took the five grand
their lives had been bountied for

and a made a face of beginning.
But demolition had crept into the bloodline,

a reliance on silence and breaking to chastise love.
Memory became the abstraction of vendetta.

Italians went to their graves without speaking,
wholly terrified of America.

Il Bambino dello sciopero

(per mia madre, mio padre e Marie)

Undici dollari alla settimana
di disocuppazione

e ancora non ero incinta.
Quando lo divenni

tuo padre iniziò lo sciopero.
Eravamo in affitto da

Nick e Ida Santilli.
Loro ci dissero non pensate all'affitto

fino a che nasce il bimbo.
Tu stavi per venire al mondo.

E tuo padre era in sciopero.
Poi arrivò l'inverno;

e, mio Dio, anche la neve;
la nevicata del 1950.

Io infornavo il pane.
Compravamo frutta e verdura dagli ambulanti.

Papà pitturava la casa di Abe e
Lena Vento.

Loro ci comprarono una culla,
perciò gli chiedemmo

di essere tuoi padrini.
Quando Papà veniva pagato

The Strike Baby

(For my mother and father and Marie)

Eleven dollars a week
unemployment

and I wasn't getting pregnant.
When I did

your father went on strike.
We were renting from

Nick and Ida Santilli.
They said forget about the rent

until the baby comes.
You were due.

Your father was on strike.
Then winter came;

and, my God, the snow:
the 1950 snow.

I baked bread.
We bought produce from the huckster.

Daddy painted Abe
and Lena Vento's house.

They bought us a crib,
so we asked them

to be Godparents.
The days Daddy got paid,

ci portava a casa
una torta da 20 centesimi.

Ci costò 110 dollari
avere un bambino:

nove mesi di gravidanza e
poi il parto,

una cura di calcio e vitamine.
Due giorni dopo che

tu eri nato,
lo sciopero finì.

he brought home
a twenty-cent pie.

It cost $110
dollars to have a baby:

nine months care
and delivery,

calcium and vitamin pills.
Two days after

you were born,
the strike ended.

Mendicante sul ponte

Da disperate sponde oltre l'Atlantico,
mando a mia madre lettere con dettagli
sull'etimologia di cirripedi e cetrioli di mare,
acuti appunti su moli e pontili.

Lei le legge seduta al tavolo di cucina,
con indosso grembiule e ciabatte,
mentre sorseggia tè come un'accigliata cinese
che cerca di puntualizzare le digressioni

del mio corsivo a mano. Si chiede perché
non scriva con le righe dritte.
Io le descrivo territori estranei.
Lei rivolta il globo per trovarmi—

ma non ci sono mai. Purtroppo il mondo
mi fa girare come un ragazzo su uno spiedo.
Alla fine della giornata lei è stanca e distante.
Le preoccupazioni l'hanno consumata come un paltò vecchio.

Ad un tratto si piega e mette in ginocchio,
trascinando poco convinta uno straccio sul pavimento di piastrelle.
L'ho punita forse troppo a lungo
con la mia incessante fame,

scambiando questo demone in cucina per una donna fantasma?
Le mie lettere sono elegie per una ragazza
disinvolta appoggiata al parafango
di un coupé bicolore, con un sedile ripiegabile,

Mendicant on a Bridge

From desperate reaches above the Atlantic,
I send my mother letters detailing
the etymology of barnacle and sea cucumber,
subtle notes of piers and bridges.

She reads these at kitchen table,
in housecoat and slippers,
drinking tea like a vexed Chinawoman
attempting to pinpoint the digressions

of my cursive hand. She wonders why
I cannot walk a straight line.
I describe unfamiliar terrain.
She twirls the globe to find me—

never there. The world turns me
sadly over like a boy on a spit.
At day's end she is tired and elusive.
Care has worn her like a coat.

On a whim she drops to hands and knees,
drags a rag skeptically across the tile floor.
Have I punished her too long
with my ceaseless hunger, ignoring

this kitchen demon for a phantom woman?
My letters are elegies to a girl
leaning cockily on the fender
of a two-toned roadster, with a rumble seat,

parcheggiato a Hoeveler Street Bridge—1937.
Lei ha uno sguardo che sospetto aver già visto,
ma mai riconosciuto.
Solo io posseggo quel ritratto

della sua segreta gioventù. La mia madre
celata, con i capelli lunghi, amabile,
per niente pratica; e, come me ora,
a mendicare sul ponte.

Il destino che ci accomuna s'è spezzato.
Viaggiamo insieme in queste lettere:
dall'Egeo al Pacifico;
qualunque mare; una nuova concezione,

una ben più straziante gestazione.
Di' loro di non cercare
la terra per me, Madre.
Me ne sono andato

verso quelle ragazze dai capelli lunghi del 1937,
un ponte ancora in piedi
integro sullo Sprofondo.
Spremerò quel ventre di pietra per una vena d'acqua.

parked on the Hoeveler Street Bridge—1937.
She wears a look I suspect I've seen,
but never recognized.
I alone possess this portrait

of her secret girlhood. My secret
mother, long-haired, lovely,
not so practical; and, as I am
now, mendicant on a bridge.

Here there is a breaking of destiny.
We travel together in these letters:
to the Pacific, the Aegean;
any sea; a new conception,

a more harrowing gestation.
Tell them not to search
the land for me, Mother.
I am gone

to long-haired girls of 1937,
a bridge still standing
uncrashed into the Hollow.
I'll bleed the stone womb for water.

Questo metallo

> *Fuori della fornace, questo metallo*
> —Thomas Bell, *Fuori della Fornace*

Lungo le rive verde scuro del fiume
distese chilometriche di parcheggi vuoti
e di vetri rotti alle finestre.

Questa la terra di mio padre.
Lassù in alto sulle prime fornaci di Carnegie,
lui è stato sospeso

sulle gru per quarant'anni
con trenta libbre d'attrezzi ai fianchi.
Vide uomini morire nelle fornaci a cielo aperto.

Da uomo del sindacato, era intoccabile.
Gli slavi non sapevano pronunciare il suo nome—
e lo chiamavano *Joe Bananas*.

Una volta in pensione, si dedica al giardinaggio
e ai fornelli e va ai loro funerali.
Ha tenuto duro per tutta la sua vita,

senza proferir parola. Quando ci fu lo sciopero
mi infilavo nella sua stanza da letto.
Non lo avevo mai visto dormire.

Il suo riposo mi spaventava:
capelli scomposti e mani vuote,
bocca spalancata, con uno sbavo di saliva,

orologio e sigarette sul comodino.
Improvvisavo dei rumori
per svegliarlo un po', al piano di sotto

This Metal

Out of this furnace, this metal.
—Thomas Bell, *Out Of This Furnace*

Along the rivers' dark green shoulders
stretch miles of empty parking lots
and broken windows.

This is my father's country.
High above Andrew Carnegie's first blast
furnaces, he swung on boom

cranes for forty years with thirty
pounds of steel on his hips.
He saw men die on the open hearth.

A Union man, he was untouchable.
The Slavs couldn't say his name—
called him *Joe Bananas*.

In his retirement, he gardens and cooks
and goes to their funerals.
He has held on all his life,

not talking. When the mill struck,
I stole time at his bedside.
I had never seen him sleep.

His repose frightened me: disheveled
hair and empty hands, opened
mouth under which widened a circle

of saliva, his watch and cigarettes
on the nightstand. I contrived noises
to wake him while on the floor below

mia madre e mia sorella con passi vellutati come fantasmi.
Quando lui aprì gli occhi, descrisse
lo sconcerto di poggiare i piedi in aria:

"Non è la caduta, figlio, ma l'improvviso arresto."
Il giorno prima aveva visto un uomo buttarsi
nel fiume Allegheny. *Un uomo vecchio,*

come lo descrisse mio padre settantenne.
Lo immagino sporgersi dalla ringhiera,
scuotere il capo, borbottare

qualcosa mentre quell'uomo, giunto prima di lui,
galleggiava verso il suo destino—
un posto che mio padre aveva spesso scorto

nelle sue arrampicate solitarie sopra
quel fuoco ora spento. Quando eravamo bambini,
aveva due vestiti buoni. Oggi anche se giorno feriale

indossa uno di quelli al funerale.
"Come l'ha presa?," chiedo a mia madre.
"Tu sai com'è fatto," mi risponde.

Poi lei scoppia in lacrime.
Lui annuisce. Ma nessuno riesce
a farlo parlare.

my mother and sister padded ghost-like.
When he opened his eyes, he described
the uncertainty of setting foot in thin air:

"It's not the fall, Son, but the sudden stop."
Yesterday he saw a man jump
into the Allegheny. *An old man*,

as described by my seventy-year-old father.
I imagine him watching
from the rail, shaking his head, muttering

something as the man, who'd beaten him
to the brink, bobbed toward his destination—
a place my father glimpsed often

in his solitary climbs above the now
vanished fire. When we were kids,
he had two suits. Today is a work day.

He is wearing one of them to the funeral.
"How's he taking it?" I ask my mother.
"You know him," she says,

then starts to cry.
He understands. But no one
can get him to talk.

Turni

Vent'anni fa, correndo verso casa
alla sirena del coprifuoco, trovai una pistola in prestito

nel comodino dalla parte di mio padre.
La città in fiamme, King era morto.

Circondato da edifici sorti dalla fatica di schiavi,
sentimmo odor di fumo venire da oltre il fiume.

I neri che camminavano lì erano domestiche e giardinieri
che mai sollevavano lo sguardo da terra;

e gli spazzini silenziosi arrivavano e andavano via
trascinando a tracolla l'immondizia prima del giorno

cantando inni che mio padre conosceva dai suoi giorni di manovale,
sgobbando su turni diurni alla fornace a cielo aperto,

e di sera lavorando da cuoco al Kennilworth.
Nella sua Rambler di seconda mano, portava i suoi compagni neri

all'acciaieria quando avevano gli stessi turni.
I suoi amici slavi della fornace lo deridevano:

un vero autista per negri. Mio padre, grazie a Dio,
andò in pensione prima della fine delle acciaierie di Pittsburgh.

Le rate della sua prima macchina nuova di zecca implacabili.
La scorsa notte, parcheggiando la Regal, è stato aggredito.

"Tre neri bastardi," mi dice al telefono.
Sta' zitto o sei morto, dissero.

Turns

Twenty years ago, I raced the curfew
siren home to find a borrowed pistol

in a drawer next to my father's head.
The city on fire, King was dead.

Surrounded by what had been built by slave labor,
we smelled smoke across the river.

The blacks who walked here were daygirls and yardmen
who never lifted their eyes from the street;

and garbage men who crept in and left
slung with our dirt before light singing

hymns my father knew from his pick and shovel days,
humping swing shifts on the Open Hearth,

and moonlighting as a cook at the Kennilworth.
In his used Rambler, he drove his black comrades

to the mill when they shared turns.
His mill-hunk buddies ribbed him:

a jitney for spades. My father,
Thank God, was pensioned before steel quit Pittsburgh.

The payments of his first new car tick against him.
Last night, parking the Regal, he was stuck up.

"Three black bastards," he tells me
over the phone. *Don't make a sound,*

Ti facciamo schizzare le cervella.
Stamattina è scivolato via dal letto coniugale

sceso in punta di piedi le scale, oltre il crocefisso,
dato un'occhiata al tempo e messo su il caffé.

Poi il suo silenzio per amore del quale
lui solo per tutti questi anni si è alzato presto.

Fuori è buio pesto—la notte incastonata
nel ghiaccio, come acciaio.

Il camion dei rifiuti s'arrampica su per la strada.
Gli spazzini con le bandane marciano verso il nostro cortile

dalla loro primitiva alba bianca.
Il sale frangighiaccio apre loro un sentiero.

I bidoni dell'immondizia rimbombano mentre sono issati.
Il sole fa irruzione dall'orizzonte gelido.

they said. *We'll blow your head off.*
This morning he left my mother's side,

tipped gently down the stairs, past the crucifix,
put an eye out for weather and started the coffee.

Then his silence for which he alone
has all these years so early risen to claim.

Outside is dark—ice, night
yet embedded in it, like steel.

The refuse truck grinds up the street.
Bandannaed garbage men march out of the white

feudal dawn into our backyard.
Rock salt burns a path for them.

Trash drums boom as they are hoisted.
The sun strikes itself on the frozen horizon.

Allarme 1° maggio

Dalla finestra della mia stanza posso con uno sputo
raggiungere la camera dei vicini Vito e Mary.
Dormivamo così tanto accanto.

Ma la furia folle della tempesta di neve del 1° maggio
colpì la loro famiglia, schiacciando Vito
a bordo della sua lussuosa Ford.

La neve traditrice infierisce, allontanando il verde
che di nascosto ammansì aprile.
Ora l'intero anno è messo a rischio.

I San Marzano di Vito pendono dai tralicci;
le azalee rosse in boccio sepolte, appassite.
Il pavimento di Mary cosparso di porcellane rotte.

L'avevo detto a quel figlio di puttana di stare a casa.
Lei strappa via il corredo dalla vetrinetta,
spegnendo Camels sulle sue cosce.

La tiara di perle troneggia nel cuscino di seta
in attesa del rito d'incoronamento. La Madonna
sorride, il serpente avvolto

ai suoi piedi di porcellana, cuore trafitto in fiamme
sul suo petto celeste. Ogni volta che Mary
agita il suo fazzoletto, i vetri gracchiano.

Nel vicolo, un paio di vagabondi
si scaldano ad un falò nel bidone.
Vito era solito cacciarli con un crick.

I ragazzini vanno con le slitte nell'antro
bianco dello Sprofondo. Sotto di loro,
la terra curva.

Mayday

From my bedroom window I can spit
on Vito and Mary's bed next door.
We slept that close.

But the freak eye of the May 1st blizzard
fixed on their house, crushing
Vito in his new Ford's plush.

Renegade snow beats down, turning back
the green that so stealthily tamed April.
Now the whole year is stunted.

Vito's Romas hang in their trusses;
azaleas buried to the red bud, withered.
Mary's floor is studded with china.

I told that son-of-a-bitch to stay home.
She sweeps her trousseau from the hutch,
stubbing out Camels on her thighs.

The pearl crown sits on its satin pillow
awaiting the coronation. The Madonna
smiles, the serpent wrapped around her

porcelain foot, impaled heart flaming
on the blue bodice. Each time Mary
lifts her handkerchief, glass crackles.

In the alley, a couple hobos lean
over a salamander. Vito used
to chase them off with a tire iron.

Kids sled into the Hollow's
white cup. Beneath them,
the earth curves.

Zia Nina sospesa in aria

Zia Nina, con la sua tuta rosa shocking,
ci accoglie alla porta, tendendoci i polsi
ingessati, fratturati
dalla sua ultima caduta.

Il Parkinson l'ha incordata come un burattino,
riducendo a spaventosi tremolii sorriso e sguardi.
Pronta al suo cenno, incorniciata dal davanzale,
c'è la badante di colore,

Gloria, che scompare
non appena ce la prendiamo in carico.
Trasferiamo zia Nina sul divano
e sediamo ai suoi piedi come facevamo un dì

da piccoli, inconsapevoli
delle *anime dei fedeli dipartiti*, quando lei tirava fuori
la storia di Spacaluccio, il mostro
di Hollow Bridge divoratore di bambini

che ci faceva correre a nasconderci nelle sue pellicce.
Lei si metteva a ridere e ci spruzzava con Emeraude spray.
Aveva guance incavate, un portamento ascetico,
la chioma blu di una regina dei fratelli Grimm.

I nostri bambini sono indifferenti.
Persi nelle loro stesse narrative,
colorano e leggono, i loro ricordi
risistemano i testi delle nostre vite.

Aunt Nina in Midair

Aunt Nina, in hot pink sweats,
meets us at the door, holding
out her casted wrists, cracked
from her most recent fall.

Parkinson's has strung her like a puppet,
spooking to staggers her smile
and gander. At her beck,
jamming the sill, is her black nurse,

Gloria, who disappears
once her charge is commended to us.
We shuffle Aunt Nina to the couch
and sit at her feet the way we used to

as kids, innocent of *the souls
of the faithfully departed,* when she'd shake
out the fable of the child-eating Hollow
Bridge monster, Spacaluccio,

that sent us tearing to hide in her fur coats.
She'd laugh and spray us with atomized Emeraude.
She had the sunken cheeks, ascetic mien,
the blue mane of a Grimms' queen.

Our children are indifferent.
Lost in their own narratives,
they color and read, their memories
rearranging the texts of our lives.

La loro prozia nubile li coccola,
mormora benedizioni, passando
su di loro la bacchetta magica della finzione
che tutto andrà bene se

rendiamo grazie a Dio, anche nelle disgrazie.
Lei stessa sembra una bambina, minuta,
il labbro inferiore imbronciato, pelle immacolata,
i capelli scostati dalla fronte

da mollette di strass.
Sulla parete sopra di lei l'incisione firmata
di Papa Giovanni XXIII.
Grasso e aquilino nel suo zucchetto di raso,

la sua grafia puntuta ex-cathedra
imprime la carta ingiallita.
Ho sentito per tutta la mia vita che zia Nina
si doveva sposare—invece di come è andata.

Vago con lo sguardo fino alle sue finestre in alto,
sotto cui sgattaiola Hill District,
ancora un tabù dalla guerra di King.
Una statua di San Benedetto il Moro

troneggia sopra gli sparuti negozi serrati
che pubblicizzano la stagione
in geroglifici Yiddish. A poche miglia lungo il fiume,
un fioco fuoco s'alza dalla fornace a cielo aperto.

Un ponte sembra affondare lentamente in acqua
tra fiamme contorte.
Per un vertiginoso istante,
capisco cosa vuol dire stare da soli

Their maiden great-aunt pets them,
murmurs benediction, passing
over them the wand of fiction
that all will be well if we

thank God, even for malediction.
She looks herself a child, tiny,
lower lip pouting, arrowroot skin,
hair fretted from her forehead

with rhinestone barrettes.
On the wall above her head is the signed
gravure of John the XXIII.
Fat and aquiline in his satin skullcap,

his spavined script tracks ex-cathedrally
over the graying paper.
I've heard all my life Aunt Nina
should have married—instead of this.

I wander to her high-storey windows,
beneath which slinks the Hill District,
still taboo from the King war.
A statue of Saint Benedict the Moor

black-lords over the spate of barred stores
hawking the season in glyphic Yiddish.
Miles down the river, pale fire leaps
from the open hearth. A bridge seems

through the distorting flame
to slowly sink into the water.
For one vertiginous instant,
I know what it's like to be alone

sospesi in aria—e non lo sopporto.
Eppure c'è della musica che proviene
dalla stanza di mia zia;
e quando entro, trovo Gloria,

ignara della mia presenza, che
suona un adagio—da quale opera non saprei dire—
sulla piccola tastiera che si regala
ai bimbi a Natale.

in midair—and I can't bear it.
Yet there's music coming
from my aunt's bedroom;
and, when I enter, I find Gloria,

oblivious to my presence, playing
an adagio—from what I couldn't say—
on a little keyboard one gives
a child for Christmas.

Saint Marie Street

Il sole inonda la stanza. Il whiskey
ribolle. La truppa di *comare* nerovestite
avanza verso Nostra Signora in rituale oscurità—

oltre il ponte di Meadow Street,
le ringhiere ora protette dopo
il primo suicidio dell'estate.

Mio padre e il mio padrino fissano
attraverso la porta con le zanzariere
la triste processione—

come scommettendo per un'assoluzione.
Versano whiskey e birra, fanno battute—
la stessa cosa di vent'anni fa,

io troppo giovane per riderci sopra—
su un tipo che ha bevuto una bottiglia intera
di Black Velvet prima di confessarsi.

La mia risata si arresta a quel punto—
ricordando Padre Dom che mi fa nero
dopo la mia prima confessione.

Dall'altra parte della strada, dei ragazzini giocano
a baseball. Le loro mazze battono sul selciato rosso
del cortile della scuola—il ritornello della mia vita.

Ero nella stessa squadra del ragazzo che è saltato giù—
mani che sembravano sfiorare appena la palla.
A diciott'anni ancora collezionava figurine,

Saint Marie Street

Sun sweeps the room. Whiskey
boils. The black-clad *comadres*
troop toward Our Lady's in confessional darkness

—across Meadow Street Bridge,
its rails now fenced
since summer's first suicide.

My Father and Godfather stare
through the screen door
at this sorrowful procession—

as if reckoning absolution. They pour
shots and beers and tell a joke—
the kind, twenty years ago,

I was too young to laugh at—
about a guy who had to drink a fifth
of Black Velvet before confessing.

My laughter has a breaking to it—
remembering Father Dom cussing me out
after my first confession. Across the street,

little boys play hardball. Their bats
carom off the schoolyard's red cobblestones—
the refrain of my life.

I was on the same team as the kid who jumped—
hands that seemed to never touch the ball.
At eighteen he still collected baseball cards,

aveva in testa il tocco di Clemente quando batteva.
Tutta la via cercava di capire perché fosse successo.
Le campane della chiesa battono *l'Angelus* di mezzogiorno.

I giocatori si inginocchiano—*un'indulgenza
di dieci* anni dal Purgatorio,
sollevano i berretti neri e d'oro dei "Pirates"

come la palla prende quota. Persino i duri
di Chookie's corner si fanno il segno della croce—
un tic nervoso a Saint Marie

dove il venerdì non si mangia carne
e gli scommettitori fanno novene.
Come pugili del tutto intronati,

i nostri padri si coprono la faccia.
D'improvviso terrorizzato dalla mia scarsa fede,
mi giro in tempo e vedo la palla volare oltre il recinto

come un'anima in fuga.
Persino questi due fedeli figli dell'esilio,
bevono senza diventare ubriachi,

immagini sacre appese alle pareti attorno—
qualunque cosa sappiano, non ce la fanno a dirla:
la loro massima aspirazione

*è azzeccare un numero
e morire nel sonno,
nel perdono.*

cocked his head like Clemente when he hit.
The whole street tried pinning it to something.
Noon church bells boom *The Angelus*.

Players fall to their knees—*an indulgence
of ten years* off Purgatory, doff
their black and gold Pirate caps

as the ball floats off. Even the hoods
on Chookie's corner cross themselves—
a nervous habit on Saint Marie

where Friday scorns flesh
and bookies make novenas.
Like punch-drunk fighters,

my fathers cover their faces.
Suddenly terrified at my lack of belief,
I turn in time to see the ball clear the fence

like a hightailing soul.
Even these two faithful sons of exile,
drinking without ever getting drunk,

holy pictures stuck to the walls around them—
whatever they know, they cannot utter:
The most you can hope for

*is to hit a number
and die in your sleep,
forgiven.*

Dalla fotografia della scalinata della chiesa, il 3 settembre 1947

Mia madre il giorno delle sue nozze
tiene stretto in mano un bouquet di gardenie.
Il profumo di quei fiori le dà alla testa,
ma lei non cede al lamento.

È la sua smorfia, col volto spostato di lato
e l'occhio sinistro un po' strizzato,
che la tradisce.
Lei fa la spiritosa sottovoce

con lo sposo, mio padre,
che le stringe la mano nella sua.
Lui sorride come sorrideva quando era
tutto preso a capire esattamente che

la perfezione non esiste.
La splendida Isabelle, damigella d'onore,
solleva lo strascico di mia madre su Meadow Street.
Accanto a lei mia nonna materna,

che indossa un cappello con dei fiori.
È regola fissa che le donne in chiesa
siano a capo coperto, e tutte quante
preferiscono quei copricapo a fiori dalle larghe falde

From the Photograph of the Church Steps: September 3, 1947

My mother on her wedding day
clutches a gardenia bouquet.
The heady flowers have her ill,
but she refuses to complain.

It's her jaw, however, set to one side,
the left eye slightly closed,
that give her away.
She's wise-cracking out of the corner

of her mouth to the groom,
my father, who has her other hand
locked in his. He smiles the way
he smiles when busy understanding perfectly

there's no such thing as perfection.
Beautiful Isabelle, the Maid of Honor,
holds my mother's train above Meadow Street.
Next to her stands my mother's mother,

wearing a hat with flowers.
It is canon that women in church
cover their heads, and all of them
favor flowery wide-brims afloat

a galla sopra i capelli lunghi. Terribilmente bello,
il testimone è Silvio Vento.
Il farfallino suo un po' storto,
e la mano infilata nella giacca del frac.

Mia madre lo disprezza: "un furbacchione,
un *gavone*." Uomo di grande fascino,
farà la sua comparsa all'improvviso
ventun'anni dopo nel giorno

della maturità di mia sorella, perché mio padre
era di turno alla fornace, e l'accompagna alla messa
per il suo diploma; poi di nuovo scompare
nel suo nascondiglio in Florida.

"Ciao, Sil," dopo tutti quegli anni:
l'unica cosa che mia madre riesce a tirar fuori di bocca.
Accalcate sui i gradini della chiesa al passaggio degli sposi
stanno le famiglie, mischiandosi in una grandinata di riso—

facce da cinegiornale, irriconoscibili
nella scolorita iconografia di questa istantanea
di quarantacinque anni fa.
Come in Bruegel, ti dà il capogiro, troppo.

Io ne so così poco. Dov'è il vestito?
Dove il garafono?
Ci sono poche foto.
La modestia dei miei genitori insolita.

Ma nell'organizzazione delle cose,
qualcosa è già fuori controllo.
In fondo a sinistra nella fotografia
c'è un uomo, di schiena, che corre

above their long hair. Dreadfully handsome,
the best man is Silvio Vento.
His bowtie is three clicks off keel,
one hand inside his tuxedo.

My mother despises him: "an operator,
a *gavone*." Man of great charm,
he will show up out of nowhere
twenty-one years later on the day

of my sister's graduation and, because
my dad is pulling shifts at the mill,
drive her to the Baccalaureate Mass;
then disappear again to his hideout in Florida.

"Hello, Sil," after all those years:
all my mother can get out of her mouth.
Filling the church steps behind the newly wedded
are the families, mingling in a hail of rice—

newsreel faces, unrecognizable
in the faded iconography of this forty-
five-year-old snapshot. Like Brueghel,
it becomes dizzying, too much.

I know so little. Where
is the dress? The boutonniere?
There are hardly any pictures.
My parents' modesty is unusual.

But in the arrangement of things, something
is already out of control. In the far left
of the photograph is a man, his back
to the camera. He rushes madly

di nuovo dentro la chiesa di Nostra Signora.
Lungo il marciapiede staziona l'auto per la luna di miele,
argentata come uno specchio al sole,
i parabrezza divisi in due da una striscia di cromo.

Colte nel vetro,
per qualche ribelle gioco di riflessi,
sono le mani degli sposi strette nel patto:
Buona fortuna, e lunga vita.

La vedo ora, solo ora
per la prima volta, l'immagine riflessa
delle loro mani intrecciate,
vedo che conoscere il futuro non gli gioverà,

e vedo anche che mio padre tiene in mano
una sigaretta consumata fino alle nocche,
vedo che lui e mia madre
stanno per prender fuoco.

back into Our Lady's. At the curb
hulks the honeymoon sedan,
in sun silvered like a mirror,
the windshield halved by a blade-length

of chrome. Caught in the glass,
by some quirk of reflection, are the hands
of the bride and groom clasped in their bargain:
Good luck. Long life.

And I see now, only *now*,
for the first time, in the image
of the image of their interlocking hands
that knowing the future will not help them,

that my father is holding a cigarette
burnt down to his knuckles,
that he and my mother
are about to catch fire.

La lingua

E la lingua è un fuoco, un mondo d'iniquità.
—S. Giacomo 3:5

Mia madre ci minacciava sempre con la sua morte.
Non camperò fino a vedere questo o quello,
o, solamente, *sarò morta per quel dì.*
Da bambino, sono certo di aver indotto quella necrofilia,
atterrito dalle sue dichiarazioni.

Ma ogni giorno che passava
imparavo quanto mendace fosse la lingua,
come invocasse vendetta, per poi tacere.
Intento a chiudermi dentro una tomba per rivalsa su di lei,
pensavo, *Dai, fallo, crepa,*
ma non parlarne più.

Un giorno mentre si vestiva—
dovevamo pagare le bollette e
non ci volevo andare—ho reagito e pronunciato
nel devastato tempio della mia testa, *affanculo*,
una parola, come *amore*, di cui ignoravo il significato,
ma che si conficcava come un chiodo,
vero come il sangue e non come semplice parola—
come la realtà del fuoco.

The Tongue

> *And the tongue is a fire, a world of iniquity.*
> —St. James 3:5

My mother used to threaten with her death.
I won't live to see this or that
or simply, *I'll be dead.*
A child, sure I had sown her death wish,
I was terrified of these utterances.

But with each day,
I learned what a liar was the tongue,
how it culled vendetta, then fell silent.
Busy bricking myself into a tomb to rival hers,
I thought, *Go ahead and die,*
but stop talking about it.

One day when she was dressing—
we had to pay bills and I was furious
about going—I turned and said
inside the ruined temple of my head,
fuck, a word, like *love*, I didn't know
the meaning of, but felt like nails,
blood-real, not word-real—
like the fact of fire.

Credevo di aver parlato tra me e me,
invece il suono di quella parola—
squallida, inconsistente, eccitante—
sgusciò strisciante fuori dalla mia bocca
creando un sussurrìo che rimbalzava nella casa.
Con addosso solo la biancheria intima,
mia madre si voltò verso di me,
afferrò un asciugamano per coprire collo e petto
in un gesto che avrei visto ripetuto
all'infinito dalle donne colte di sorpresa.

Incapace di negarlo,
rimasi fuori la sua camera da letto,
la punta della parola ancora appesa alla mia bocca
come un coltello a serramanico.
D'un tratto, per rappresaglia per la vergogna provata,
avrei voluto essere morto.
Sapevo che la sillaba troncata era equivalsa
ad una confessione segretamente fatta
a me stesso minuto per minuto
ogni giorno della mia vita.

Non avrei potuto immaginare
tutti quegli anni fa—ero soltanto un ragazzino—
cosa quella parola significasse.
Guardando mia madre che in silenzio
arretrava nella sua stanza e fuori dalla mia vita—
come se stesse per sfondare la finestra
e andare svestita verso la bufera di neve,
separandosi da me per sempre—
era chiaro che
anche lei ne era ignara.

I'd thought I'd been talking to myself,
but the sound of that word—
cheap, weightless, thrilling—
wormed out of me in a voice
which the house over and over whispered.
In only her underthings,
my mother wheeled, clutched for cover
a towel to her throat and breast
in a gesture I would see
astonished women forever copy.

Unable to deny it,
I stood outside her bedroom door,
the tip of the word still hanging
like a switchblade from my mouth.
Suddenly, to punish her for the shame I felt,
I wanted to be dead.
I knew that clipped syllable had amounted
to the confession I had been secretly making
to myself minute by minute
every day of my life.

I couldn't possibly have known
all those years ago—I was just a little boy—
what that word meant.
Looking at my mother as she backed mutely
into her room and out of my life—
as if she were about to crash unclothed
through the window into the snowstorm,
leaving me once and for all—
it was clear
she too was innocent of it.

L'elettrizzante vernacolo della fuga

Da ragazza, Marie leggeva così tanto
che mia madre l'aveva bollata come pigra,
un'accusa pesante in una famiglia
di lavoratori incalliti. A modo suo,
la mamma era calvinista.
Credeva nella mortificazione della carne,
che indeboliva la volontà.
Il lavoro ti tiene lontano dalle tentazioni.
Non è niente, le piaceva ripetere alle nostre proteste,
ringraziate il Signore che avete braccia e gambe.

Ogni pagina che Marie girava,
ogni volo dell'immaginazione,
descriveva un'impronta rimasta sul tappeto,
un piattino sporco sulla credenza,
il giornale abbandonato sull'ottomana.
Le parole possedevano un disordine mirato,
senza modestia, nere come i *Negri*,
violando il primigenio ricamo della pagina.

Mia sorella, pallida, occhialuta,
spaparanzata sopra il letto, un libro
come un neonato fra le braccia,
atterriva mia madre; come se
nelle sue incessanti letture avesse dato vita
alla mamma contro il suo volere:
maledetta e imperdonabile, asservita
a mantenere una casa dove le parole
come topi sgusciavano dal battiscopa,
a cascata tra gli argenti, sprofondando dopo di sé

The Electrifying Vernacular of Escape

As a girl, Marie read so much
my mother branded her lazy,
a withering accusation in our house
of ceaseless toil. In her way,
Mother was a Calvinist.
She believed in mortifying the flesh,
denaturing will.
Work took your mind off things.
It's nothing, she liked to say of our discomfort.
Just thank God you have both arms and legs.

Each page Marie turned,
each flight of make-believe,
described a stray footprint on the carpet,
a dirty saucer on the sideboard,
the newspaper left overlong on the ottoman.
Words possessed a focused untidiness,
immodest, black as *Negroes,*
violating the pristine doily of the page.

My sister, pale, bespectacled,
disarrayed cross her bed, a book
like an infant splayed in her arm,
terrified my mother; as if
in her incessant reading she had authored
Mother against her will: cursed
and unforgivable, lashed
to keeping a house where words like mice
burst from the woodwork,
tumbled among the silver, dropping

la punteggiatura del rimpianto,
il traslato amaro della memoria.

Adeguandosi ai voti del silenzio ed obbedienza,
Marie non rispondeva nulla.
Chiudeva il libro,
ci metteva il segno con il santino della Madonna,
e avanzava rispettosa per la casa
come una prigioniera destinata alle pulizie,
lustrando porcellane, strusciando linoleum,
lisciando le lenzuola sfatte dei letti,
qualsiasi compito le ottave ad alta voce di mia madre richiedessero.
Eppure quel libro, come un amante proibito,
sussurrava dal suo nascondiglio,
adescandola con le sue promesse
di pericolosa seduzione:
l'elettrizzante vernacolo della fuga.
Era soltanto una questione di tempo prima che lei
di nuovo scivolasse tra quelle pagine, per scomparirvi dentro.

behind them the punctuation of regret,
the bitter trope of memory.

Adhering to vows of silence and obedience,
Marie said nothing.
She closed her book,
clipped its place with a holy card of the Virgin,
and pressed dutifully through the house,
like a captive forced to char,
scouring porcelain, mopping linoleum,
redding the soiled linen from the beds,
whatever homage the raised octaves of my mother required.
Yet that book, like a forbidden lover,
whispered from its hiding place,
luring her back to it with promises
of seduction and danger:
the electrifying vernacular of escape.
It was just a matter of time before she slipped
into its pages and disappeared.

Silenzio

> Il silenzio è un tratto di famiglia.
> Un certo nostro antenato dev'esser stato un solitario—
> un grand'uomo circondato da dementi, o un povero illuso—
> che ha insegnato ai suoi discendenti questo silenzio.
> —Cesare Pavese, "Mari del Sud"

Negando che in me risieda il sonno
sprofondo nel fresco cotone
del letto di mia nonna, ultraterreno,
che profuma di gigli e pelle appena strofinata.
Racemi di sicamoro, i frutti appena germogliati,
grattano alla finestra, spandendo
lampi di luce sulle mie lenzuola.
Un ragazzo sperduto in un torrione immacolato,
io non sogno, ma sono sognato,
certo che i miei occhi non si siano mai chiusi;
eppure l'albero ha dispiegato la sua ombra sulla stanza
per un'ora, la luce, un bagliore conico come il raggio di un proiettore,
adesso sulla maniglia bianca di porcellana della porta,
che si gira fino a lasciar la presa, rivelando
nella cornice spoglia dello stipite
il mio defunto nonno sarto
in un vestito d'invisibile fumo.
Lui avanza, con le mascelle serrate,
le mani nascoste dietro la schiena, fino al mio letto,
e guarda verso di me in giù lentamente.
Il suo volto grigio scricchiolando si rivela. Finalmente,
finalmente, mi sta parlando.
A quel suono tento di sollevarmi,
ma sono un nato morto,
relegato al Limbo, senza un nome.
Cosa mi sta dicendo?
Non so distinguerlo.
Poi lui si volta indietro,
la mani offese cucite l'una all'altra.

Silence

> *Silence is a family trait.*
> *Some ancestor of ours must have been a solitary man—*
> *a great man surrounded by halfwits, or a poor, crazy fool—*
> *to teach his descendants such silence.*
> —Cesare Pavese, "South Seas"

Denying there is in me sleep
I lay in the cool cotton deep
of my grandmother's otherworldly bed
that smells of lilies and freshly scrubbed flesh.
Sycamore racemes, just come to fruit,
paw the window, fanning
sunbursts over my sheets.
A lost boy on a spotless keep,
I do not dream, but am dreamt,
sure my eyes have never closed;
yet the tree has bent across the room
an hour of its shadow, the light,
in a conical gleam like a movie ray,
now on the white porcelain doorknob,
turning until released, revealing
in its naked jamb
my dead tailor grandfather
in a suit of invisible smoke.
He walks, lock-jawed, hands hidden
at his back, to my bedside,
and looks down slowly.
His gray face grinds open. Finally,
finally, he is speaking to me.
I try to rise to the sound of it,
but I am stillborn,
pinned in Limbo, unnamed.
What is he saying?
I can't make it out.
Then he turns his back,
snubbed hands sewn to each other.

Melanzana

Così tante volte mi ci son trovato
che "familiarità" non è la parola

per evocare il gesto di mia madre
in assalto su quella forma di seno nero-violacea,

il suo coltello che la sbuccia a partire dall'areola,
strisce di pelatura nel lavello

finché il corpuscolare ortaggio diventa nudo
pronto per essere affettato. Nel colino

dispone i dischi circolari, salando ogni strato
per estrarre l'umore amaro, e poi

li pressa con un ferro a forma di cuore—
che suo padre da sarto usava.

Stazionano sul ripiano tutto il giorno:
la melanzana e sopra la sua pressa a cuore,

il liquido nel tegame sottostante
che diventa vermiglio.

Eggplant

So many times I've witnessed this
that *familiarity* is not the word

to conjure my mother's taking up of the breast-
shaped purple blackness, her paring

knife commencing from the areola,
strokes of peel stripping into the sink

until the corpuscular fruit is nude
and ready to be sliced. In the colander

she tiers the rounds, salting each layer
to draw out the bitter water, and weights

them down with a piece of heart-
shaped iron with which her tailor father pressed.

They sit on the counter all day:
the eggplant with the heart pressing on them,

the water in the pan beneath
turning red.

Maria Roselina

C'è un momento della domenica,
un inspiegabile istante di lucidità e
intenzione che i morenti spesso adducono,
in cui mia madre dalla nebbia allunga una mano,
si solleva dal letto e avanza verso la cucina.

Sul ripiano di marmo, mescola uova e farina,
sale e acqua, lavora il sudario dell'impasto,
la riduce a strisce di tagliatelle,
e poi ricopre il tutto con un panno.

Persino la pioggia si ferma e spunta il sole
per favorire il suo passaggio verso l'orto
alla volta di pomodori, prezzemolo,
aglio e basilico.

Così quando in punta di piedi entriamo
nel silenzio anestetizzato della casa dei miei,
nel lungo pomeriggio di un respiro
e poi un respiro in meno,
odoriamo la salsa e ci arriva dallo stereo
Connie Francis che canta *Al di là*.

Nella sala da pranzo: lunghi e ancora caldi
filoncini di pane Siciliano; il servizio buono
posizionato per il primo e il secondo,
il rallentato confortevole rituale della tavola;
la luce, come il giorno cala, accende
nelle caraffe il purpureo chianti.

Con la schiena rivolta verso di noi, mia madre
in piedi ai fornelli. Al suo fianco,
mio padre grattugia il pecorino,

Maria Roselina

There is a moment Sunday,
an inexplicable instant of clarity
and purpose the dying often summon,
when my mother extends a hand through the mist,
lifts off her bed and makes for the kitchen.

On a marble slab, she mixes egg and flour,
salt and water, rolls flat the shroud of dough,
snips it into *tagliatelle*,
and covers it with a sheet.

Even the rain halts and the sun appears
to allow her passage into the garden
for Romas, parsley,
garlic and *basilico*.

So that when we tiptoe into the etherized hush
of my parents' apartment,
and the long afternoon of one breath
and then one breath less,
we smell the sauce and hear Connie Francis
from the stereo singing *Al Di La*.

In the dining room: long still-warm
loaves of *Siciliano;* china
stationed at each place for *primi, secondo*,
the unhurried, comforting office of the table;
light, as day latens, flaring
in pitchers of purple chianti.

Her back to us, my mother
stands over the stove. At her side,
my father grates *Pecorino*,

ricambia i nostri sguardi attoniti con un sorriso:
lo sapeva dall'inizio che lei si sarebbe ripresa.

Nella grande pentola argentea che
abbiamo adorato per tutta la nostra vita,
l'acqua con la pasta
ribolle come un oracolo.

Mia madre vi sbircia dentro, mescolando:
poi si gira per salutarci:
grembiule rosso, perle, tuta da casa,
scarpe da tennis bianche per signore fuori moda.
Profeticamente,
eleva il mestolo di legno.

Dietro di lei, colonne di vapore
s'alzano e posano
nei suoi capelli bianchi
come simulacri.

parries our looks of astonishment with a smile:
he knew all along she'd snap out of it.

In the large silver pot
we have worshipped all our lives,
water with the pasta
roils like an oracle.

My mother peers into it, stirring;
then turns to greet us:
red apron, pearls, sweatpants,
old-fashioned ladies white tennis shoes.
Prophetically,
she elevates the wooden spoon.

Behind her, columns of steam
rise and roost
in her white hair
like little statues.

Domenico Giuseppe

Pescato dalla lunga fila in coda
presso la sicurezza all'aeroporto,
il mio novantenne padre collabora con slancio,
quasi amabilmente; affatto sorpreso, sembrerebbe,

che il caso lo abbia prescelto
per rispondere su qualcosa di cui è innocente.
Due prosperose matrone in uniforme,
capelli raccolti e cinturone di pelle nera lucida,

distintivo d'argento a forma di cuore,
gli chiedono
se ha accettato nulla da estranei
da quando è entrato nel terminale.

Lui assicura loro che non accetta mai nulla
da sconosciuti. Lo scrutano come se
la sua affabilità fosse uno stratagemma,
un filamento avvitato alla bomba che detonerà.

Lo scandagliano con un metal detector,
gli sfilano il cappotto, scuotono il suo bastone.
Lui sorride loro e le chiama "signorine."
Gli intimano di togliersi le scarpe,

un paio di Adidas bianche,
immacolate senza un graffio; il suo cappello,
una vecchia fedora marrone, lo rovesciano
a ripetizione, svuotandolo del suo niente,

Domenico Giuseppe

Singled from the queue filing
through airport security,
my 90-year-old father is fully cooperative,
even amiable; not even surprised, it seems,

that fate has tapped him on the shoulder
to answer for something he is innocent of.
Two uniformed buxom matrons,
coiled hair and black patent leather

Sam Browns, heart-shaped
silver badges, ask him
if he's accepted anything from strangers
since he's entered the terminal.

He assures them he never accepts things from strangers.
They study him as if his affability
is part of the ploy, a filament
wired to the bomb he'll trigger.

They prod over him an electric wand,
slip him out of his overcoat, shake his cane.
He smiles and calls them *young lady*.
He's ordered to remove his shoes,

a pair of white Adidas,
not a scuff upon them; and his hat,
an old brown fedora they flip over
and over and empty of its nothingness,

prima di palparlo come un carcerato,
ascelle e inguine, scorrendo le loro mani
su e giù per gambe e braccia,
su tutte le ossa dello scheletro e giunture

come se per magia potesse smembrarsi
e rivelare la vòlta segreta dell'Armageddon.
Improvvisamente mio padre è il terribile Isaia.
Eppure persiste il suo sorriso, persino mentre lo spogliano,

lui barcollante svestito e scalzo sui suoi piedi gialli,
peli bianchi che stanno per prendere fuoco nel suo torace,
gambe da capomastro blu tungsteno,
mentre si sente distintamente provenire da lui un tic.

Poi lo scuoiano,
lo squarciano con un coltello a scatto:
filamenti sconnessi, fuoriusciti,
prese sigillate, fili fermati col nastro—

i misteriosi circuiti della detonazione.
Ancora non trovano quello che stanno cercando,
e lui non riesce a ricordare
dove l'ha nascosto.

before patting him down like a convict,
armpits and crotch, sliding
their hands up and down his arms and legs,
each skeletal ridge and knob

as if by magic he might divide
and reveal the vault of Armageddon.
Suddenly my father is terrible as Isaiah.
Yet he remains smiling, even as they strip him,

tottering naked on bare yellow feet,
white hair smoking off his chest,
millwright-legs tungsten blue,
from him emanating an audible tick.

Then they peel him out of his skin,
jackknife him open:
sprung, mis-spliced wires,
capped sockets, taped frays—

the mysterious circuitry of detonation.
Still they don't find what they're searching for,
and he can't remember
where he's hidden it.

Il cappello di mio padre

Mio padre aveva una fedora color marrone.
Da bambino, amavo

odorarne l'interno,
la corona foderata di seta

con il suo stemma:
due grifoni alati che reggevano

uno scudo decorato con la sontuosa scritta
New York, che combaciava

con la sommità della sua testa;
poi lo scudo era sigillato con una fodera lucida

come se conservasse
in una camera recondita un reliquario:

i denti canini di S. Tommaso D'Aquino,
il cuore ancora pulsante

di Thomas Becket,
un qualche segreto che mi chiedeva pegno

in quanto figlio di mio padre
per questo copricapo sacro.

My Father's Hat

My father owned a soft brown fedora.
As a child, I loved

to smell the inside of it,
the satin-lined crown

with its coat of arms:
two winged gryphons clutching

between them a shield flourished
with *New York*, against which

crested the roof of his head;
then sealed with glassy

batting, as if chambered
within lay a secret reliquary:

the eye teeth of Aquinas,
the still beating heart

of Thomas Becket,
some secret tithing me

as my father's son
to this sacred hat.

Il venditore ambulante

Le donne di Prince e Omega Street
accorrevano a frotte nel campo DiDomeni
quando *Cesare*, Caesar, il mercante zingaro,
arrivava col suo camioncino rosso vivo
da cui fuoriuscivano prodotti favolosi,
piantine di calendule e begonie,
orchidee *Cymbidium*, gelato al limone,
frutti di sambuco, occasionali bottiglie magnum
di champagne Florentine, e
quando di stagione, lepre marinata.

Sembrava un Paladino, un Caravaggio,
ciò che io, appoggiato ad un parafango,
mentre rubavo uva verde, riconoscevo
come un viso crudele, sudicio di peluria,
baffi malandrini come in un film muto,
ogni sua mossa squisitamente coreografata,
come un mago dal nulla fa spuntare
albicocche, nettarine e pesche
con il colorito delle ragazze irlandesi—
anche se vestito come un contadino abruzzese,
fazzoletto bianco avvolto intorno al collo,
un crocefisso d'oro pendente dalla sua catena, una fedora nera. Aveva
accoltellato dei frequentatori a Larimer Avenue
per le carte e le ragazze.

Le donne, in abiti estivi sbracciati,
cascate di capelli raccolti col foulard,
con i borsellini pieni di spiccioli—così anche mia madre—
s'affrettavano a contrattare l'ultima cassetta di ciliegie e
prugne, impilate, sgocciolanti succo sanguigno
nel piatto della sua bilancia, l'ago che impazziva
come un contatore Geiger.

The Huckster

The women on Prince and Omega streets
flocked to DiDomeni's Field
when *Cesare*, Caesar, the gypsy huckster,
arrived in his bright red pick-up
spilling gorgeous produce,
flats of begonias and marigolds,
Cymbidium orchids, lemon ice,
elderberries, occasional magnums
of Florentine champagne,
and, in its season, dressed hare.

He looked like Paladin, Caravaggio,
what I, hanging on a fender,
stealing green grapes, recognized
as a cruel face, filthy with stubble,
rakish silent movie mustache,
his every move exquisitely choreographed,
as if a wizard, spinning out of thin air
apricots, nectarines, peaches
with the complexion of Irish girls—
though dressed like an Abruzzi peasant,
white kerchief tied at his neck,
gold crucifix on its chain, black fedora.
He'd knifed johns on Larimer Avenue
over cards and girls.

The women, in sleeveless summer dresses,
fountains of hair scarved at their crowns,
change purses—my mother too—hurried
to haggle over the final crop of cherries,
damson plums piled dripping, bloody
in the pan of his scales, its needle
jouncing madly like a Geiger counter.

Una volta che le aveva sotto il suo incanto,
rivelava un bottino di sigarette di contrabbando,
radio a transistor, album di dischi.

Le calze di seta le teneva nascoste fino alla fine,
come se le avesse fatte comparire dal nulla,
e possedevano il potere di trasformare
le nostre madri in vere regine.
Lui ne apriva una scatola,
estraeva il sottile tubolare,
ci infilava il pugno dentro e tirava su la guaina
fino a tutto il muscoloso braccio.
Attraverso la filatura trasparente
grossi peli neri spuntavano magicamente—
a riprova del suo potere incantatorio specie sulle donne,
dimostrando che tutto con lui poteva succedere:
affari d'oro, inimmaginabile lusso,
e anche trasformare il braccio di un ambulante
nella gamba carnale di una bestia.

Once he had them in his sway, he revealed
his cache of dirt-cheap hot cigarettes,
transistor radios, record albums.

The silk stockings he withheld
until last, as if he'd conjured them,
and they possessed the power to turn
our mothers into queens.
He'd open a package,
tear out a flimsy gauntlet,
rustle his fist through its mouth,
and sheath it up his rippling arm.
Through the transparent weave
thick black hairs magically sprouted
—as if proving his powers,
especially over women,
that he could make anything happen:
bargains, unimaginable luxury,
transform a huckster's arm
into the carnal leg of a beast.

Le sorelle DeNinno

Una foto d'artista in bianco e nero
ritrae mia madre e le sorelle
al banchetto delle Christian Mothers,
presso The Embers in East Liberty—
la data *18 febbraio 1947*
impressa in rosso porpora nel retro—
sedute ad una tavola imbandita di lino bianco, bouquet di gardenia,
argenti, porcellana,
cristalli, corpetti, sigarette
surrettizie in posaceneri d'opalina.

Potevano essere in attesa dell'Eucaristia,
aspettando di essere rapite, macellate
per la fede, eppure mia madre e le zie
non avevano preso l'ostia
dal giorno del matrimonio. Unico uomo ammesso,
il fascinoso pastore gesuita,
Padre Beatrix, davanti a lui
una boccetta di scotch Inver House
e un accendino Scripto con le sue iniziali
per le sue Lucky Strike, con il bersaglio rosso
sul pacchetto: il cuore di Maria Immacolata.
Le donne della parrocchia ne sono tutte innamorate:
collare bianco immacolato, la copia spiccicata
di Charles Boyer, in *Gaslight*—
affascinante, sofisticato, accento alsaziano.

Lo stuolo di suore del pastore,
le Sorelle della Divina Provvidenza,
un ordine tedesco, ugualmente lo adora.
Abiti prussiani, neri come la pece, sorridono
dai ritrosi cerchi occhialuti del soggolo.
Mia madre e le zie le chiamano *bestie*.

The DeNinno Sisters

A black and white studio portrait
documents my mother and her sisters
at the Christian Mothers banquet,
The Embers in East Liberty—
Feb. 18, 1947
stamped in purple on its back—
at a table frothed in white linen,
gardenia compotes, silver, china,
crystal, corsages, cigarettes
demurring in milk-glass ashtrays.

They could be waiting for the Eucharist,
waiting to be ravished, slaughtered
for the faith, yet my mother and aunts
have not indulged in the sacraments
since Matrimony. The only man permitted
is the handsome Jesuit Rector,
Father Beatrix, before him
a cruet of Inver House
and monogrammed Scripto
for his Luckies, red bull's-eye
on the package: Mary's Immaculate Heart.
The parish women are in love with him:
blinding Roman collar, spit and image
of Charles Boyer, in *Gaslight*—
charming, urbane, Alsatian accent.

Father's bevy of nuns,
Sisters of Divine Providence,
a German order, also worship him.
Prussian habits, black as wire, they smile
from the prim bespectacled caves of their wimples.
My mother and aunts call them *beasts*.

Beatrix, il vice di Dio, il *playboy*,
si crede Cristo in persona.
Le DeNinno l'hanno sgamato.
Solo un idiota oserebbe indisporle
nei loro perentori abiti stizzosi.
Loro sfidano chiunque a metter bocca.
Ma, cristallizzate in questa posizione
nella foto, in posa, raggianti,
non faranno mai una piega, né potranno
quel silenzio assoluto abbandonare per l'eternità.

Beatrix, the Christ-proxy, the *playboy*,
thinks he's the Christ.
They have his number too.
Only a fool would cross them
in their imperious pissed-off dresses.
They dare someone to mouth off.
But, immured at their stations
in this photograph, posed, beaming,
they'll neither flinch nor abandon
their perfect silence forever.

Messa della domenica

Nelle domeniche d'inverno,
quando mio padre era in sciopero dalla fonderia,
lui e mia madre si svegliavano tardi,
poi s'alzavano e preparavano per la messa domenicale
a SS. Pietro e Paolo.

Rifugiandomi nella loro stanza,
mi arrampicavo sul letto di ciliegio a quattro colonne
che avevano comprato da May Stern
il mese prima di sposarsi, nel 1947—
ancora caldo dei loro corpi, col loro odore,
la vasta spasa di trapunta
e coperte che mi avvolgevano.

Mia madre, in sottoveste, davanti alla toletta,
mi guardava mentre io guardavo lei allo specchio.
Le sopracciglia arcuate, la bocca leggermente aperta,
la lingua che passava sopra il labbro superiore—
nel modo in cui le donne inconsciamente
atteggiano il volto quando si truccano—
sfoltiva le arcate e colorava il viso, spazzolava all'infinito
i suoi lunghi capelli castani,
applicava sulla bocca il suo rossetto dall'astuccio dorato,
e premeva le labbra rosse in un bacio.
Attorno al collo chiudeva un giro di perle,
inclinando la testa, affondava nei lobi gli orecchini,
scivolava dentro il vestito e poi chiamava
il nome di mio padre, *Joe*, che le tirasse su la zip.

Scuro, rasato di fresco,
lui stava davanti al comò
dove tenevano le polizze dell'assicurazione,
i certificati dei vaccini, le buste segrete—

High Mass

Winter Sundays,
when my father was on strike from steel,
he and my mother woke late,
then rose and prepared for high mass
at Saints Peter and Paul.

Wandering into their room,
I climbed into the four-poster cherry bed
they bought at May Stern
the month before marrying in 1947—
warm from their bodies, their scent,
its voluminous spread
and blankets enveloping me.

My mother in a slip, at her vanity,
watched me watch her in its mirror.
Eyebrows arched, mouth slightly open,
tongue dabbing at her upper lip—
the way women unconsciously arrange
their faces when making-up—
she plucked and painted, brushed
forever her long brown hair,
circled her mouth with a golden tube of lipstick,
and pressed her red lips together in a kiss.
Around her neck fastened pearls,
dipped each ear to earring,
slipped into her dress and called,
Joe, my father's name—to zip it.

Dark, clean-shaven,
he stood at the bureau—
where they kept insurance policies,
immunization records,

a scegliere la cravatta e il fazzoletto.
La sua camicia bianca aveva il polsino alla francese e i gemelli di rubino.
Mi sorrideva.
E appena le aveva tirato su la lampo del vestito,
allacciava la sua cravatta di seta rossa,
senza neppure guardare,
in un perfetto nodo.

Mia madre, che era sarta, lo ispezionava,
poi sistemava il risvolto del suo abito blu.
Lei cuciva i vestiti per mia sorella.
Quelle mattine, mio padre a casa,
non c'era fretta e non venivamo scontentati.
Mangiavamo uova e pancetta,
e via verso la chiesa nella Plymouth.
Marie ed io avevamo imparato sin da piccoli
a non varcare mai un picchetto.

secret envelopes—
choosing a necktie and handkerchief.
His white shirt had French cuffs, ruby cufflinks.
He smiled at me.
That quickly he had her fastened,
his red silk tie looped,
without even looking
into a perfect four-in-hand.

My mother, a seamstress, inspected him,
then patted his blue suit lapel.
She made my sister's clothes.
Those mornings, my father in the house,
we weren't rushed and resigned.
We ate eggs and bacon
and rode to church in the Plymouth.
Marie and I learned as children
never to cross a picket line.

Involtini

Con l'artiglio del martello
di ferro battuto—reso lucido
come l'argento dalle infinite
fiammate di fuoco, forgiato
a Manfredonia, Puglia,
da mio nonno
fabbro ferraio, Paolo
Battiante, arrivato
sulla nave *Luisiana*,
dalla provincia di Foggia,
nel 1907, a Ellis Island,
dove il suo cognome fu storpiato,
come quello di tanti altri,
il martello nascosto sotto la giubba—
mia madre sbatte
su un tagliere da macellaio
fettine di carne tenera da marinare,
poi ne cosparge ogni strato con olio d'oliva,
aglio, prezzemolo, sale e pepe,
prima di ridurle in involtini
legati con lo spago
comprato alla panetteria Stagno,
gettando poi il tutto
nella rubiconda maestà
del sugo a rosolare
per il resto della nostra vita.
Amen.

Braciole

With the cast iron claw
hammer—burnished
silver in endless
bouts of fire, forged
in Manfredonia, Puglia,
by my blacksmith
grandfather, Paolo
Battiante, arrived
on the *Luisiana*,
out of the province of Foggia,
1907, Ellis Island,
where his name was altered,
like so many, the hammer
secreted in his tunic—
my mother pounds
on butcher block
flank steak to temper,
then layers each pliant tongue
with olive oil, garlic, parsley,
salt and pepper, before
trussing them into scrolls
bound with string
from Stagno's Bakery,
and dropping them
into the incarnadine
majesty of the sauce to roil
the rest of our lives. Amen.

Concertina

Alias filo spinato, concepita
come lo strumento a fiato ad ancia libera,
con rigonfiamenti a fisarmonica, brevettata

nel 1844 da
Sir Charles Wheatstone. All'inizio della sua storia,
il *Volo del Calabrone*

di Rimsky-Korsakov fu arrangiato per
la concertina inglese.
Usata come bastione difensivo nella Prima Guerra mondiale.

Avrete visto foto d'archivio
di soldati ancora penzolanti, abbandonati, appesi come fantocci
tra le sue spire.

Un semplice filo spinato guarnito di eliche attorcinate
a forte trazione, di vari calibri e tipi di lame,
un colossale Uomo a Molla Slinky

infiocchettato di bisturi
che tagliano al tempo stesso in alto e in basso.
Una fisarmonica all'italiana.

I nomi dei manifatturieri come *Excalibur, Flight-Guard, Whistler,
Nemesis, il Prodigale*—concepiti in modo tale che,
una volta catturato, il prigioniero di riflesso

Concertina

Alias razor wire, fashioned after
the free-reed,
bellows-drive instrument, patented

in 1844 by
Sir Charles Wheatstone. Early in its history,
Rimsky-Korsakov's

Flight of the Bumblebee was arranged for English
concertina.
Used as ramparts in WWI. You've seen

archival photographs
of soldiers dangling still, lovelorn, as puppets
in its trusses.

Simple barbed wire garnished with spun helices of high
tensile yield,
various calibers and blade profiles, a colossal Slinky

ribboned with scalpels
that incise vertically and horizontally at once.
An Italian squeezebox.

Manufacturers' names like *Excalibur, Flight-Guard, Whistler,
Nemesis, The Prodigal*—
so conceived that, once snared, the convict, reflexively

si agita forsennato (preso dal panico
mentre gli s'infila dentro), s'attorciglia su se stesso
come in un trita carne.

Al sole pieno e al chiaro di luna, particolarmente seducente.
L'intermezzo,
l'emorragia al suo culmine.

thrashing (panicked
as it flinches into him), ravels himself through
a meat grinder.

In the sun and moonlight, especially seductive.
The intermezzo,
the climactic hemorrhage.

Per Frank O'Hara

La prima volta alla 24esima Est—
abbiamo un attico, interno 117—
a Gramercy Park, piove.
Dai vetri di un negozio di alimentari,
vediamo l'acqua della pioggia scendere,
il marciapiede diventare scuro.
Mangiamo dolmades e diamo una scorsa ai giornali,
decidiamo per una retrospettiva su Jacob Lawrence
anche se capiamo di non farcela.
Il Metropolitan Museum chiude alle cinque e mezzo.
Senza ombrello, c'incamminiamo sotto la pioggia,
per qualche isolato, fino a Curry Hill,
con la sua sfilza di ristoranti indiani.
Incollati ai pali telefonici
i poster che pubblicizzano *Corpi: In mostra*.
Uomini scuoiati, cadaveri,
interiora incartapecorite rosse, bianche e blu,
denudati interruttori con fili elettrici spellati,
come colori d'acquerello si dissanguano nell'acquazzone:
mazze da golf sferranti, jogging, corpi in corsa,
palloni da calcio imbracciati,
più determinati, più allegri, dei viventi.
Approdiamo nel locale The Curry Leaf:
pakoras e samosas con piccante chutney all'albicocca,
birra Kingfisher e budino di riso.
La deferente grazia del cameriere di Madras,
il tovagliolo bianco appoggiato sul braccio,
ciotole d'acqua per pulirsi le dita. Fuori del ristorante,
un cambogiano vende piracanta, gladioli,
garofani tinti, nebbiolina,
orchidee *Cymbidium* vulviformi.
Propone bouquet ai passanti sotto la pioggia.
I taxi giallo vivo in coda riluccicano.

For Frank O'Hara

The first day on East 24th—
we have a loft, #117—
in Gramercy Park, it rains.
Through a delicatessen window,
we watch the water fall,
the sidewalk darken.
We eat dolmades and scour the papers,
decide on a Jacob Lawrence retrospective
we know we'll never make.
The Met closes at 5:30.
No umbrella, we walk a few blocks
in the rain to Curry Hill,
its cadre of Indian restaurants.
Slapped to telephone poles
are posters advertising *Bodies: The Exhibition*.
Skinned men, cadavers,
leathery red, white and blue insides,
denuded circuit boxes, stripped,
like water colors, bleed in the downpour:
swinging 9 irons, jogging,
bolting up-field, cradling footballs,
more determined, more cheerful, than the living.
We settle on The Curry Leaf:
pakoras and samosas with fiery apricot chutney,
Kingfisher and rice pudding.
The deferential charm of the Madras waiter,
the white cloth across his sleeve,
finger bowls. Outside the restaurant,
a Cambodian sells Fire-thorn, Gladiolus,
dyed carnations, Baby's Breath, vulviform
Cymbidium orchids.
He hands bouquets to people passing in the rain.
Bright yellow the queued glistening cabs.

Luce alla vena

Questo è l'aldilà
soglia dell'oblìo:
una cresta d'asfalto
su Pine Mountain,
Bell County, Kentucky,
la Statale 119 che attraversa
ardente a nord il cuore
del carbone finché non si sfinisce,
dal gelo, a DuBois, Pennsylvania.
Dalla nebbia velata di lavanda,
il sole che si è risvegliato
in vestimenti bianchi va in estasi:
Gesù affiancato da Mosè
ed Elia, trasfigurato,
*su verso una montagna alta
lassù*. Giù in profondità
i minatori prendono fiato,
puntano la luce alla vena.

Light at the Seam

This is the afterlife,
threshold of oblivion:
a blacktop crest
on Pine Mountain,
Bell County, Kentucky,
US Route 119 burning
north through the heart
of coal until it plays out,
frozen, in DuBois, PA.
Out of gauzy lavender fog,
the wakened sun
swoons in white robes:
Jesus, flanked by Moses
and Elijah, transfigured,
*up into a high mountain
apart.* Deep within,
miners suspire,
shake light at the seam.

Limbo

In *Quasi paradiso*,
la fotografia di Carl Galie—
scattata dalla posizione del
Cielo—finalmente ho contezza
del Limbo, esattamente come me lo figuravo:
un'infinita distesa dell'inveterata catena
dei monti Appalachi, proprio le cime,
nella lucentezza autunnale,
fino al loro mento in nubi d'ovatta,
un suggello d'insondabile bianco
da qui a Ninive.
Il Limbo è invero *quasi Paradiso*—
ma decisamente non proprio il Paradiso—
dove i bimbi non battezzati,
in fiamme perenni
per il Peccato Originale, sono destinati,
per l'eternità, a non guardare mai
la fronte di Geova—
sebbene il catechismo ci tranquillizzi
che non soffrono,
felici in quell'altitudine
tra gli infiniti
pixel del firmamento
che li tiene in fasce, esclusi,
tra le nuvole—l'aldilà
creato il giorno secondo.

Limbo

In *Almost Heaven*,
Carl Galie's photograph—
composed from the vantage
of Heaven—I finally witness
Limbo, precisely as I pictured it:
an endless sweep of the ancient
Appalachian chain, just the peaks,
in autumnal brilliance,
to their chins in cottony vapor,
an imprimatur of fathomless white
from here to Nineveh.
Limbo is indeed *almost Heaven*—
but decidedly not Heaven—
where unbaptized babies,
ever-smoldering
with Original Sin, are sentenced,
for eternity, never to gaze
upon the brow of Yahweh—
though Catechism confirms
they're not in pain,
happy at this altitude
among the infinite
pixels of the firmament
swaddling them, excluded,
in clouds—the afterlife,
created on the second day.

Acknowledgments

Grateful acknowledgment is extended to the following presses and journals in which some of these poems, in some cases different versions, first appeared:

"Paolo Mio," "Sempre Fidele," "Larimer Avenue," "A Better Life," "Grazziella," "The Headstone," "Lincoln Avenue," "Prometheus," "Son of a Priest," "Confirmation," "Kyrie," "The Hollow," "The Witch," "The Death of East Liberty," "The Strike Baby," "Mendicant on a Bridge," "This Metal," "Turns," "Mayday," "Aunt Nina in Midair," "Saint Marie Street," and "From the Photograph of the Church Steps: September 3, 1947" from the volume, *This Metal* (Press 53, Winston, Salem, NC, 2012).

"The Tongue," "The Electrifying Vernacular of Escape," "Silence," "Eggplant," "Maria Roselina," "Domenico Giuseppe," and "My Father's Hat" from the volume, *Restoring Sacred Art* (Star Cloud Press, Scottsdale, AZ, 2010).

"The Huckster," "The DeNinno Sisters," and "Braciole" from the volume, *The 13th Sunday after Pentecost* (Louisiana State University Press, Baton Rouge, LA, 2016).

"Concertina" from the volume, *Concertina* (Mercer University Press, Macon, GA, 2013).

"Limbo" from the volume, *Light at the Seam* (Louisiana State University Press, Baton Rouge, LA, 2016).

"For Frank O'Hara" in *RSAJournal* (*Rivista di Studi Americani, Journal of AISNA / Italian Association of North American Studies, 28/2017*).

About the Author

JOSEPH BATHANTI is the former North Carolina Poet Laureate (2012-14) and recipient of the North Carolina Award in Literature, the state's highest civilian honor. The author of over twenty books, Bathanti is McFarlane Family Distinguished Professor of Interdisciplinary Education at Appalachian State University in Boone, North Carolina, and is the recipient of the Board of Governors Excellence in Teaching Award. He served as the 2016 Charles George VA Medical Center Writer-in-Residence in Asheville, NC, and is the co-founder of the Medical Center's Creative Writing Program. His volume of poetry, *Steady Daylight*, from Louisiana State University Press, is forthcoming in 2026. He was inducted into the North Carolina Literary Hall of Fame in October of 2024.

About the Translators

MARINA MORBIDUCCI, PhD, Associate Professor in English Language and Translation at Sapienza University, Rome, lectures at MA and Specialized Translation Master Courses. Her research focuses on translation of contemporary American poetry. She published first Italian editions of works by Robert Creeley, Charles Olson, Kathleen Fraser and Gertrude Stein (*Tender Buttons, Last Operas and Plays, Lifting Belly*, etc.). As a recipient of a Fulbright scholarship at State University of New York at Binghamton, she was Prof. William V. Spanos' student and collaborated with the journal of postmodern literature *boundary 2;* she also contributed to *How2*, a journal of women's innovative writing. Her first academic publication in American experimental writing dates back to 1987, with an anthology on Black Mountain College - poetry and poetics, providing the first Italian translation of "Projective Verse." Her latest monograph on G. Stein's notion of time is titled: *Gertrude Stein in T/tempo. Declinazioni temporali nell'opera steiniana*. (http://www.editricesapienza.it/node/7897, 2019).

A native New Yorker and Yale graduate, DARCY DI MONA has been in Rome for forty years, working as a teacher and professional translator in the field of the arts. She has translated art catalogues, event programs, articles on architecture, interviews with artists, film directors and producers, and even the epic history of an Italian tuna company. Back in 2006, she started translating the catalogues and websites of what are now three Italian film festivals, while teaching English at several Roman universities, and until recently directed a translation workshop at Rome's Sapienza University, which produced Italian versions of André Acimen's marvelous descriptions of Roman alleys by night in *Call Me by Your Name*, among other fare.

CROSSINGS
An Intersection of Cultures

Crossings is dedicated to the publication of Italian language literature and translations from Italian to English.

Rodolfo Di Biasio. *Wayfarers Four*. Translated by Justin Vitello. 1998. ISBN 1-88419-17-9. Vol 1.

Isabella Morra. *Canzoniere: A Bilingual Edition*. Translated by Irene Musillo Mitchell. 1998. ISBN 1-88419-18-6. Vol 2.

Nevio Spadone. *Lus*. Translated by Teresa Picarazzi. 1999. ISBN 1-88419-22-4. Vol 3.

Flavia Pankiewicz. *American Eclipses*. Translated by Peter Carravetta. Introduction by Joseph Tusiani. 1999. ISBN 1-88419-23-2. Vol 4.

Dacia Maraini. *Stowaway on Board*. Translated by Giovanna Bellesia and Victoria Offredi Poletto. 2000. ISBN 1-88419-24-0. Vol 5.

Walter Valeri, editor. *Franca Rame: Woman on Stage*. 2000. ISBN 1-88419-25-9. Vol 6.

Carmine Biagio Iannace. *The Discovery of America*. Translated by William Boelhower. 2000. ISBN 1-88419-26-7. Vol 7.

Romeo Musa da Calice. *Luna sul salice*. Translated by Adelia V. Williams. 2000. ISBN 1-88419-39-9. Vol 8.

Marco Paolini & Gabriele Vacis. *The Story of Vajont*. Translated by Thomas Simpson. 2000. ISBN 1-88419-41-0. Vol 9.

Silvio Ramat. *Sharing A Trip: Selected Poems*. Translated by Emanuel di Pasquale. 2001. ISBN 1-88419-43-7. Vol 10.

Raffaello Baldini. *Page Proof*. Edited by Daniele Benati. Translated by Adria Bernardi. 2001. ISBN 1-88419-47-X. Vol 11.

Maura Del Serra. *Infinite Present*. Translated by Emanuel di Pasquale and Michael Palma. 2002. ISBN 1-88419-52-6. Vol 12.

Dino Campana. *Canti Orfici*. Translated and Notes by Luigi Bonaffini. 2003. ISBN 1-88419-56-9. Vol 13.

Roberto Bertoldo. *The Calvary of the Cranes*. Translated by Emanuel di Pasquale. 2003. ISBN 1-88419-59-3. Vol 14.

Paolo Ruffilli. *Like It or Not*. Translated by Ruth Feldman and James Laughlin. 2007. ISBN 1-88419-75-5. Vol 15.

Giuseppe Bonaviri. *Saracen Tales*. Translated Barbara De Marco. 2006. ISBN 1-88419-76-3. Vol 16.

Leonilde Frieri Ruberto. *Such Is Life*. Translated Laura Ruberto. Introduction by Ilaria Serra. 2010. ISBN 978-1-59954-004-7. Vol 17.

Gina Lagorio. *Tosca the Cat Lady*. Translated by Martha King. 2009. ISBN 978-1-59954-002-3. Vol 18.

Marco Martinelli. *Rumore di acque*. Translated and edited by Thomas Simpson. 2014. ISBN 978-1-59954-066-5. Vol 19.

Emanuele Pettener. *A Season in Florida*. Translated by Thomas De Angelis. 2014. ISBN 978-1-59954-052-2. Vol 20.

Angelo Spina. *Il cucchiaio trafugato*. 2017. ISBN 978-1-59954-112-9. Vol 21.

Michela Zanarella. *Meditations in the Feminine*. Translated by Leanne Hoppe. 2017. ISBN 978-1-59954-110-5. Vol 22.

Francesco "Kento" Carlo. *Resistenza Rap*. Translated by Emma Gainsforth and Siân Gibby. 2017. ISBN 978-1-59954-112-9. Vol 23.

Kossi Komla-Ebri. *EMBAR-RACE-MENTS*. Translated by Marie Orton. 2019. ISBN 978-1-59954-124-2. Vol 24.

Angelo Spina. *Immagina la prossima mossa*. 2019. ISBN 978-1-59954-153-2. Vol 25.

Luigi Lo Cascio. *Othello*. Translated by Gloria Pastorino. 2020. ISBN 978-1-59954-158-7. Vol 26.

Sante Candeloro. *Puzzle*. Translated by Fred L. Gardaphe. 2020. ISBN 978-1-59954-165-5. Vol 27.

Amerigo Ruggiero. *Italians in America*. Translated by Mark Pietralunga. 2020. ISBN 978-1-59954-169-3. Vol 28.

Giuseppe Prezzolini. *The Transplants*. Translated by Fabio Girelli Carasi.
2021. ISBN 978-1-59954-137-2. Vol 29.

Silvana La Spina. *Penelope*. Translated by Anna Chiafele and Lisa Pike.
2021. ISBN 978-1-59954-172-3. Vol 30.

Marino Magliani. *A Window to Zeewijk*. Translated by Zachary Scalzo.
2021. ISBN 978-1-59954-178-5. Vol 31.

Alain Elkann. *Anita*. Translated by K.E. Bättig von Wittelsbach.
2021. ISBN 978-1-59954-170-9. Vol 32.

Luigi Fontanella. *The God of New York*. Translated by Siân E. Gibby.
2022. ISBN 978-1-59954-177-8. Vol 33.

Kossi Komla-Ebri. *Home*. Translated by Marie Orton.
2022. ISBN 978-1-59954-190-7. Vol 34.

Leopold Berman. *The Story of a Jewish Boy*. Translated by Giuliana Carugati.
2022. ISBN 978-1-59954-192-1. Vol 35.

Alain Elkann. *Nonna Carla*. Translated by K.E. Bättig von Wittelsbach.
2021. ISBN 978-1-59954-201-0. Vol 36.

Luigi Pirandello. *Man, Beast, and Virtue*. Translated by Alice Roche.
2024. ISBN 978-1-59954-205-8. Vol 37.

Maria Teresa Cometto. *Emma and the Angel of Central Park*.
2023. ISBN 978-1-59954-157-0. Vol 38.

Alain Elkann. *A Single Day*. Translated by K.E. Bättig von Wittelsbach.
2024. ISBN 978-1-59954-211-9. Vol 39.

Elisabetta Rasy. *The Indiscreet*. Translated by Siân E. Gibby.
2024. ISBN 978-1-59954-212-6. Vol 40.

www.ingramcontent.com/pod-product-compliance
Lightning Source LLC
Chambersburg PA
CBHW030856170426
43193CB00009BA/626